PRAISE FOR FREE & EASY...

Free and Easy: How to Create Your Own Adventure by Living on the Road uses the term *on the road* as a metaphor for bringing significant changes into your life and is based upon what the author learned when he left his corporate job at the age of 49 for a more independent existence. The book is about recognizing and organizing resources available to you to create a more independent life. One person who had the opportunity to read the book while it was still a work in progress had this to say.

"When I first heard of this book my thought was that it would be a good travelogue, a collection of entertaining stories. Little did I realize the practical applications it contained for me and my family.

"I was working, had a good job and worked for a great boss. I am a 25 year diabetic and although I had some problems with the disease two years earlier it took a turn for the worse in late 2002. I faced disability and I was caught unprepared.

"My wife and I read this book in earnest, wondering if after 30 years in the corporate world...would we survive. Could I start a new, healthier life? We answered the questions the book posed honestly. We did a complete review of finances, applied the practical lessons and we made the transition to a healthier, simpler, much improved lifestyle. We are finally doing what we have always wanted to do.

"This book is an important step in your personal direction. I would encourage you to read it and understand."

STEVE HANNER (June 2004)

Another person, who had the opportunity to read the book while it was in development and who has had an independent life himself as the author of many outdoor books had this to say about *Free and Easy: How to Create Your Own Adventure by Living on the Road.*

"Most of us sooner or later must confront the nagging sense that our lives could be more rewarding, more meaningful, or at least, more fun — if only we weren't stuck in our present circumstances. In our cubicles or offices, in our cars while commuting or in airport terminals on business trips, we look at our lives and wonder what possibilities might await us if only we could get out of here and go out there.

"David Ryan knows this feeling well, but unlike most of us, David and his wife, Claudia, did something about it, and in this engaging, informative, and inspirational book David explains how others can too. He chose the phrase life on the road as a metaphor for the kind of self-directed life he's talking about, a metaphor not for rambling around in an RV—though that's a legitimate option — but rather for living life as an exciting journey.

"I've enjoyed knowing David for several years; we've hiked and explored together and shared many conversations in coffee shops. He's not a wild-eyed utopian but rather a down-to-earth practical guy who has worked and succeeded in business, been a parent, and had the same mundane concerns and responsibilities as the rest of us. That's what makes this book so valuable: David demonstrates that living life on the road not only is desirable but also is possible. Skillfully blending information with inspiration, he explains how he and others have been able to achieve this.

"Many years ago, when I was a young English major, I encountered some lines by the English poet Matthew Arnold that have accompanied me on my own journey through life:

> 'And the rest, a few,
> Escape their prison and depart
> On the wide ocean of life anew.'

"Life is indeed a wide ocean, and if we truly wish to travel more freely upon it, this book can help us to weigh our anchors and hoist our sails."

BOB JULYAN (July 2004)

FREE & EASY

FREE & EASY

*How to Create
Your Own Adventure
by Living on the Road*

A guide for changing your life

David Ryan

FIRST EDITION 2004

10 9 8 7 6 5 4 3 2 1

LIBRARY OF CONGRESS CATALOG CARD NUMBER: 20044096823
ISBN: 0–938631–29–2 paper

ALSO BY DAVID RYAN:

Long Distance Hiking on the Appalachian Trail for the Older Adventurer

BOOK DESIGN/PRODUCTION: Sunny Elliott, SunFlower Designs of Santa Fe
TYPEFACE: Goudy Oldstyle, Goudy Sans

PUBLISHED BY:

PENNYWHISTLE PRESS
1807 Second Street, Suite 28
Santa Fe, New Mexico 87505
pennywhistlebook@aol.com
www.pennywhistlepress.com

*For Claudia who has been there and
continues to be there for the journey "on the road."*

CONTENTS

ACKNOWLEDGMENTS

I must acknowledge that the restlessness stirred within me by Henry David Thoreau's **Walden** has been a driving force in my life ever since I read it for the first time while in high school. Since Thoreau's experiment on Walden Pond occurred one hundred years before I was born, it would be difficult for me to give him the credit for making this book possible. For that, I must thank my wife Claudia, my daughters Jennifer and Amy, and my friends Bob Julyan, Steve Hanner, Victor di Suvero, John Holden and Nancy Adam who contributed many ideas and kept me pointed in the right direction. I am especially grateful for the many hours of meetings in the Page One Bookstore Coffee Shop over the past two years with Bob Julyan to discuss personal independence and what would be important to cover in the book. I would also like to thank the many people who unknowingly helped me create this book by their responses to ideas I bounced off them during casual conversations. I would also like to thank the Pennywhistle team for turning this manuscript into a book. Without all of these contributions this book would not have been possible. Finally I cannot close this discussion without acknowledging Frank and Aimee Hilliard who have taught Claudia and me so much about values and philosophy and their application to everyday living.

FOREWORD

by *Stephen C. Joseph, MD*

Want to pedal your bike from Bangkok to Katmandu? Sail your yacht around the Horn to Tahiti? Hitchhike from Alaska to Machu Picchu?

This book won't tell you how to do any of that.

What it will tell you is how to get your personal affairs, your mind, and your resolve into shape so that you can live *on the road* —whatever road that is: mundane and familiar, exotic and far-away, or any combination that suits you. While he's at it, the author drops some pearls of practical advice about personal effects, finances, mail, and keeping in touch with those home folks not fortunate enough to be on the road with you.

All of us Americans have been on the road since we got here, and always will be. The First Americans hauling their fur skins and sledges across the Land Bridge, and then continuing over millennia to spread out, north to south and west to east. African captives in the holds of slave ships, or, later, following "the Drinking Gourd" to some hoped-for freedom. My European grandparents, and perhaps yours, coming up from steerageway to kiss the ground at Ellis Island, then moving beyond with ten cents in their pockets. More recently, but just the same, from Guatemala and Mexico, Viet Nam and Laos, and Somalia and Tibet, and from a hundred other places in a hundred other languages, they keep coming. And may they keep coming forever.

Once here, the road seduces us, draws us on and on. Dan'l Boone keeps moving when he sees the smoke of his neighbor's cabin chimney. Sweet Betsy from Pike goes Westward Ho. Woody Guthrie rides the rails, Jack Kerouac and Easy Rider criss-cross back and forth. All our best songs, and all our best stories, are fundamentally about *Living on the Road.*

The passion, the compulsion, to be *on the road* is our most seminal national characteristic, seemingly built into our DNA (Don't Never Arrive. Just keep on truckin').

Well, in this 21st Century, many of us, maybe, have to sublimate a bit. Can't go with Ol' Dan'l through the Cumberland Gap. Can't ride the Pony Express with Bill Cody. Can't burn our way out to that Big Rock Candy Mountain and the Lemonade Springs Where the Bluebird Sings. But the compulsion is there, deep in our bones, and under our skins, none-the-less.

So David Ryan tells you how to make do with what you can— no small accomplishment in this Age of Compromise. Maybe not for Always, maybe just for a Season. Maybe not Over the Rainbow, maybe just back to where you went to high school.

That's not bad, not by a long shot. Helps you scratch the itch. Gives you a glimpse, and a feel, and a share of the courage your ancestors reached down for when they actually got on that boat, probably never to look back.

David Ryan doesn't give you, nor sell you the dream. That part is up to you. He eases you down the road, helps you to figure out for yourself just how far you want to go—this time. Maybe next time go a little further. Keep a bridge or two from burning. Share the road with your partner. "Hold fast to dreams," as Langston Hughes said. Because when you are walking down that road, however narrow and near it is at the moment, you can see a long, long way beyond.

INTRODUCTION

by *Victor di Suvero*
Publisher, Pennywhistle Press

FREE & EASY by David Ryan is really more than one book. Within its covers the various aspects of building a new life for one's self, with or without a partner, shine with simple clarity. As a well cut stone reflects its light from each of its many facets, each chapter translates itself into separate meaningful elements, all of which, when taken together, make it a jewel of a book.

The premise on which *Free & Easy* was built is that there is another way of living one's life, a way other than the standard nine to five format that has become a hallmark of our current commercial economic middle class structure. We live in a world where business has developed a work force ethic that serves its corporate requirements within finite parameters that have become more and more stringent over the past fifty years.

Each section of the book stands alone while each one deals with separate but important elements that have to do with the various decisions that must be made in order to be responsible in financial, familial and practical terms. The fact that David Ryan's wife Claudia has played an integral role in their own decision making process, as well as in the implementation of the vision they had for their future, cannot be minimized.

Though the concept of trading job security for their adventure — their "life on the road" — may seem risky and even foolhardy to many readers, the book is a chronicle of their success in stepping off "the moving sidewalk" they were on. As David says "when you can separate yourself from the noise, you may discover that much of what you worried about and the passions that consumed you were really quite trivial. You may look back at many of the so called "crises" at work and realize that they were about nothing, and were more often than not caused by someone wishing to demonstrate their firefighting skills." The concepts and attitudes presented in this book can even be of service to people who may never want to take all of the steps to begin their own journeys "on the road." By examining their own lives in terms of the adventure the author and his wife dared to implement as a way of life for themselves, they have achieved a better life for themselves. Many readers will find interesting and exciting ways of enhancing their own lives even while staying within the safety and comfort of their current employment situations.

The book's importance is based on two principal issues — it does show how an alternative to an unsatisfactory employment situation can be created in a reasonably risk free manner while at the same time it manages to provide a gateway to adventure that is not usually considered a realistic possibility in our commercially structured society today. Filled with personal reflections as well as with innumerable pieces of practical advice *Free and Easy* manages to merge the idea of practical responsibility with the basic appetite for adventure that is part and parcel of the American dream.

David Ryan's open and engaging style makes it possible for the reader to enter into a world that is not usually considered easily accessible. He does this in an orderly and competent manner that will enlarge the reader's horizons if not actually change his or her life.

What This Book Is About

"I'm gonna check out of this bourgeois motel.
Push myself away from the dinner table
and say 'No more Jell-O for me, Mom.'"

from the movie **Peggy Sue Got Married**

There may be a good chance that you have thought about checking out of your *bourgeois motel* and going *on the road* yourself. When thinking about the expression *on the road* your first thought may be of Jack Kerouac and friends zooming around the country hopped up on who knows what in a flurry of hedonistic self absorption; or perhaps, it is of Dennis Hopper and Peter Fonda riding their motorcycles across the country in **Easy Rider**; or maybe, your image is of a Charles Kurault-type TV news story about visiting some cute "old timey" corner of the country where the lemonade is cold in the summer and the kids are polite all year round. These are certainly images of the road, but on a more personal and positive level *on the road* could be about releasing yourself from the constraints of the conventional work world to have time to explore other interests, or making the time to do the one thing—or *many* other things—that you cannot possibly consider doing right now.

It really comes down to being able to set your own agenda and doing something because you *want* to do it rather than because you *ought* to do it, or to paraphrase Peter Fonda in **Easy Rider**, *"doing your own thing in your own time."* This book is not a collection of *oh wow* stories from the road nor is it a sales pitch for you to go *on the* *road.* This book — ***Free and Easy: How to Create Your Own Adventure by Living on the Road*** — is about what you can do to make your life more interesting and uses the expression *on the road* as a metaphor for bringing significant changes into your life.

I can write about this from experience because when my wife, Claudia, was 48 and I was 49, we sold our house, stored our possessions, quit our jobs in Chicago and took off to live literally on the road for two years. After two years on the road we returned to a more conventional, but still independent, lifestyle in New Mexico to take on new challenges. So for us, our on-the-road experience has had (to date) a distinctly literal phase and also a separate metaphorical phase. In both cases we discovered that the same planning and thinking process that worked for one also applied to the other.

You may be picking up this book because you have thought about doing the same, or at least doing something different than what you are doing right now. When I was in your position I would read whatever I could about breaking away. Unfortunately, I found most of the books and articles to be about as valuable as sprinkling pixie dust on the top of my head to make life better. The authors would tell me about their fabulous fast track lives or the inner demons that they had to cope with in making their choice. Or, they would tell me that if I dreamed hard enough all the money I would ever need would miraculously fill my pockets. Some suggested that if you were cunning enough you could get your boss to give you all the time off you needed to get your head together. I recently saw an article on the Internet saying that you could ask your parents to give you an advance on your inheritance to fund some time off. (Let's assume that we are adults here using our own resources to make this happen.) Other writings turned out to be a re-hash of personal journals that were about as fascinating as a four-hour slide show of someone's holiday getaway to their weekend cabin. That's not this book.

Claudia and I were not on any corporate fast track and had

long recognized that we had jobs rather than careers. There is not enough mystery in "my-story" to warrant your interest. It is your story that is important, not mine. This book is a compilation of what we have learned while being on the road that could be of value in your planning and action. In the process of sharing these lessons, I will often fall back on how they applied to us as to evidence of their value. That is as close as I want to get to telling my story.

Of course, if you like your life just the way it is and have no interest in changing, then don't. But if you are at a point in your life where you desire something different and want a certain sense of adventure, this book may have some merit in helping you make a change. If you choose to change, you will not be alone. The call to close up shop and move on has been part of the American psyche since its inception. This continent would not have been settled without the willingness from the very first Native American to the most recent immigrant to take a risk. The call was also heard by those who no longer wished to live, or act, in a conventional manner. Daniel Boone, Henry David Thoreau, Thomas Merton, some entrepreneurs, and many others are in that group. You may be so frustrated with what you are doing right now that you are ready to join them too.

Even if you would like to join them immediately and know that an independent course is the right or only choice for you, you could have too many obligations or not enough money in the bank to make the move right now. That doesn't mean that you can never be independent, it just means that you will have to wait. But by knowing what you want now you have an advantage and can get a head start on your preparation. That was certainly my situation, as it was several years after I made the commitment that I was actually able to do it. And remember if you never start the process, you will never do it.

But be warned: Living on the road is not for the timid. It involves risk and change, especially if you choose a path that means loosening bonds to your current life and responsibilities to wander about the world. However, it could also mean quitting your job and staying put to change careers or to adopt a dramatically different lifestyle. Or, it could end up being a combination of lifestyle and location changes to do something entirely new. Regardless of what *the road* means or will mean to you, it involves your willingness to take the risk of stepping out on to your own path without knowing exactly where it will take you. And this willingness to take a risk leads to the next important concept of the book title — personal adventure. Anytime you bring in change or a degree of uncertainty into your life, it opens up the possibility of adventure. Change could be an opportunity to make your life more interesting to you. The only question remaining is if creating your own adventure by living on the road is a good choice for you.

If you do make the move, being *on the road* may only be a transitional period in your life, or it may become a permanent change. It may take on many forms. It could be making time to become more contemplative and to process what you have learned throughout your life to better understand life in general. It could be following Thomas Merton into a monastery. (If you are not familiar with Thomas Merton, you may be interested in reading his **Seven Story Mountain** on why he moved to the monastery or **New Seeds of Contemplation** on what he learned from living in a monastery.) It could be making time to learn a new skill for a completely different career, or to satisfy a lifelong curiosity. Or, it could be as simple as going for a series of experiences and personal adventures to engage more fully in life. Making the move and how you use your time is your decision. Ultimately, it comes down to whether you intend to turn your talk into action or not.

The opportunity to become more contemplative while on the road should not be overlooked. Becoming more reflective can have a religious/spiritual aspect. But for those more secular it is really about finding the time that's often unavailable in a more conventional life for quietness. Then you can open yourself up to all that's around you. If you are able to open yourself, you may at sometime truly see all there is and come to realize how wonderful the world is and how fortunate you are to be part of it. If that happens, it can profoundly change you because that insight will come from deep within you, and you will recall that moment for years to come. For many, to have that type of experience requires that they be totally in the present; that is, completely divorced from the worry of what happened yesterday and from the anticipation of what will happen tomorrow. It is difficult to be in the present when you are caught up in the conventional world of work and noise. The opportunity to get away from the noise is what the road is all about.

When you can separate yourself, you may discover that much of what you worried about and the passions that consumed you were really quite trivial. You may look back at many of the so-called "crises" at work and realize that they were about nothing, and were more often than not caused by someone wishing to demonstrate their firefighting skills. At a more global level, you may recognize that so many of the passions that consume society have been based upon fear and were reactions to threats that were only imagined. One of your challenges in your journey *on the road* will be finding a balance in your life to try to separate the noise from the substance. A good step in that direction is to recognize that most of what we do has the same impact as sticking one's finger in a glass of water. As the water returns to its level when you pull your finger out, the world will go on whether you are here or not. It is right at this very moment that you have impact.

As humankind's way of living has shifted from hunting and gathering to subsistence level agriculture and then to our present world of commerce and industry, many of us have become separated from the natural rhythms that governed living for millennia. In this progression, many of us have become separated from living in and with nature and have managed to divorce the consumption of the goods and services we use from their actual production. As a result, many of us have now become so specialized that we are likely to be completely dependent on other people for everything we use. Certainly, there have been many positive benefits from this ever increasing complexity in the way we live; however the demands of a complex social system have made it difficult for us to slow down and disengage from worry. The opportunity to recapture the natural rhythms of life and spend time in the present is also what the road is about.

The shift from a self-sufficient farmstead economy to a commercial/industrial economy was beginning to accelerate during Henry David Thoreau's time. His experiment in self-sufficient independent living at Walden Pond was a reaction to that shift. When he was talking about the rail line that skirts the edge of Walden Pond as riding upon us rather than us riding upon the rails, he was talking about an economy that continues to this day to ride upon us to the point where we are so dependant upon our jobs that for many any hope for sustenance, health care, or an adequately funded retirement is at risk without one. Stepping back from a complex omnipotent economy and moving to a simpler life closer to nature is for some what the road is about.

Before moving on, I do want to mention that there is another very popular type of *on the road* experience — the retiree living fulltime in their RV while traveling around the country. Although this book could have value to anyone contemplating change in their life, and certainly does have tips on sustaining a mobile existence, this book is not an instruction guide on fulltime RV living. There are already many guides available for that. This writing is directed to those in their middle and later middle years, who have had enough of the work world and are ready to do something different, or metaphorically speaking ready to live *on the road.*

Each person will have to come to their own interpretation of what being *on the road* should be. These decisions will be influenced by personal health, family and financial circumstances combined with personal goals, dreams and interests. An *on the road* experience could take on several phases and many ways of being. Some phases could be literally spent on the road accomplishing tasks that could not normally be pursued within the constraints of a normal vacation period. Regardless of your interpretation, there will be some basics regarding decision making, financial planning, and establishment of infrastructure that will apply to all modes of being *on the road*. Those who will still need income will have to expand their interpretation to include income producing activities. All of these items and more are discussed in this book.

Ultimately, making the break to live *on the road* will involve a process of

- Self examination

- Understanding what you want to do

- Financial planning

- Preparation, and

- Learning

This is what this book is about.

The one thing I can tell you is that if you are able to make the break and put yourself in a position to pursue lifelong dreams, you will not regret it. Our literal two years on the road remain a valued and peak experience for us. The exhilaration of being free from needing (or wishing, if you are out of job) to go to work on Monday and having an open future in front of you is difficult to describe. My uncle, who once took two years off from working, told me several years later that those were still the two best years of his life. Another person I know who also lived literally on the road for over a year after heart surgery, said that that time away from work saved his life. In my case more than five years after settling into a more conventional setting, I can recall to the day every place I went and everything I did during those two years. In the subsequent five years, we have engaged in enough income-producing activities that keep the lights on without taking too much time away from pursuing many new and life long goals. If you are serious about doing the same, you will find that there is a life outside of the conventional work world, and it can be great. The success of your experiment will be up to you.

Deciding for "the Road"

Limestone karst peaks in the farming country and lake area near Yangshuo, China. Photographs by the author.

*"You don't think yourself into a new kind of living;
you live your way into a new kind of thinking."*

20th Century Catholic theologian, **Henri Nouwen**

In order to start living your way *into a new kind of thinking,* you will need to start with three basic steps. The first is to make the decision to look into the possibility of change. It is one thing to shoot your mouth off about how lousy work is; it is a completely different thing to see what you can do about it. The second step is doing the necessary research to determine if it is possible or feasible to bring change to your life. You are now getting closer, but until you make the change it will still only be talk. It is the third and final step of actually doing it that will separate you from those who talk about changing and place you with those who actually do.

In my case, I had always visualized doing something outside the conventional work world. I had difficulty taking the corporate world seriously and was restless being a part of it. I had made several stabs at getting out of it. Unfortunately, I was unsuccessful. There were, however, a series of events that helped me move from the first step and on to the second and third steps.

Like many young people I had spent a lot of time sitting around with friends talking about what I would do when I became rich and successful. Most of the people around me thought they would be millionaires by the time they reached forty. When I reached forty and was not a millionaire, I wanted to know why. I sat down and made a spreadsheet of my missed opportunities—poor job choices, poor investment decisions, the cost of broken marriages, and others. By the time I added it up, I found out that with a few adjustments I could very well have been a millionaire by the time I was forty.

What had started out as a joke and a mild diversion had now become a sobering experience. At first I beat myself up for being a knucklehead. But I quickly realized that if I had had that many at bats before the age of forty, think of how many more chances I would have over the rest of my life. It didn't mean that I would recognize them or handle them any better; it just meant that at the age of forty there was still plenty more to come and plenty of time to do different things with my life. What the exercise helped me realize was that I had to be more aware of what I really wanted if I was to break away from the drift-and-dream cycle that I was in.

Very soon after completing the spreadsheet, my youngest sister and I were on a two week trip to China. We were traveling independently and meeting many people who built their life around travel and personal adventure. On a boat trip down the Li River amidst the scenic limestone karst peaks from Guilin to Yangshuo, we met an English couple from Gibraltar, in their middle 40's, who had been to every corner of the world. Rather than taking a bus back to Guilin to hurry on to their next stop and eventually back to work as we were, they were going on to the southwestern Chinese backcountry to learn about tortoiseshell plastrons. They were in no hurry and on no timetable. They were going to spend as much time as they wanted to on this pursuit. I have no idea what a tortoiseshell plastron is, but it seemed more interesting and more important than the unending "blame-storm" meetings, hollow slogans, and pushing air waiting for me back at work.

I had found my heroes. They were not leisure class millionaires; they were normal people who worked construction for six months or so to build up enough money to take off for extended travel. When their funds ran out, anywhere from three to nine months later, they would go back to Gibraltar to start the cycle again. What I learned is that there are people who are not rich, who do what they want by investing in their experiences rather than in their lifestyle. I realized that that was what I wanted — the ability to blend supporting myself financially and creating enough off time to pursue interests outside of work.

There were also little events that reinforced my desire to get out of the regular work world. One was when my daughter and I were visiting the Grand Canyon. We had not been able to get a backcountry permit for the time we would be there to hike to the bottom and spend the night inside the canyon. We had to be content with hiking half way down and back out within a day. Although it is not the same as spending the night in the canyon, a day hike in the canyon is still a wonderful experience. While at the canyon we learned that there are oftentimes backcountry permit cancellations and that we would probably get a permit if we could wait two or three days. Again, I had to get back to work and could not wait. This was another wake-up call on the need to get out of the position of having to get back and to put myself into the position of having the time to go ahead.

Another small event occurred when I was between jobs and actually had time to play a game of tennis on a weekday. It was a perfect, and extremely rare, late summer day — cool, clear and sunny, and definitely not typical for Chicago. Afterwards, my tennis partner and I were commenting on what a great day it was and noting that our lives were too short to keep living in an area with such bad weather. I realized that devoting my life to earning a living was not only limiting what I could do; it was also keeping me in an area where the year-round outdoor activities that I liked to do were very restricted.

Just before I actually made the break I discovered another insight. This happened when I was on a business trip with a colleague. While we were driving from the airport to our appointment, my colleague was talking about time he spent in Alaska before he

Claudia's Motivations for Seeking Independence

Our decision to leave our jobs and declare independence was not made unilaterally by me; it was a joint decision. It was not a case of my coming home from work one day and announcing that we were selling the house and moving to a backwoods hut. We both had our motivations and worked together to make our independence a reality. I have discussed some of my motivation in the narrative, and I have asked Claudia to share her motivation and perspective.

Well, we both did plan and agree to leave the mainstream work world, but I never would have done this without David's ideas and motivation. I had for many years been aware that while the company I worked for appreciated my skills they didn't particularly like my personality. I'm a loner and in the age of networking and empowerment I pretty much stood out like the proverbial sore thumb. Until I met David, I just kept trying to fit in, with not much success. So in many ways the lifestyle change has been the answer to my prayers. I can choose opportunities to use the skills that the work world valued in ways that are more important to me. I read and process information constantly; I've taken up the violin for a new challenge; I have volunteered in church, political, and social service organizations — still looking for the right one to use my talent and for me to get fulfillment; I run, hike and do yoga to keep healthy (hopefully); I've healed a broken leg and have gone through breast cancer surgery with chemotherapy and radiation following. Life continues to have its ups and downs, but now I'll never have to regret not having seen the United States (just two states left) or spending time with family and friends. I've learned more about life (and Life) in the past eight years than in the 47 before. I have the opportunity now to live with fewer distractions and so to acknowledge what my life is about.

joined the Air Force and went to Viet Nam. As he was talking about the mountains, the snow, the bears, and driving on black ice in Alaska, it hit me that when many people are relaxed and engaged in casual conversation, they talk about what they did in the service or what they did before they were overwhelmed with personal responsibilities. Rarely do you hear anyone talk about their adventures in the business world and what a great meeting they had. It helped me further realize that, if you are fortunate, there may be a time when you have taken care of enough of your personal responsibilities that you can then take the time to become the person you were meant to be.

But perhaps the final and most compelling reason for me to embrace change was how I felt every time I returned from an annual industry conference or trade show. My jobs in various sales and marketing positions required me to attend and exhibit at occasional trade shows/conferences. As you start going to these types of events on a regular basis you begin to spot people from other organizations and continue to see them a few times a year on an on-going basis. After a few years of this it seemed to me that no one was really developing; they were just getting older. It was just a repackaging and recycling of the same old, and getting older, stuff. After years of self-denial it eventually sunk into me that I was no different. When I woke up to that dose of reality, I asked myself if this was really what I wanted to do and if this in any way resembled what I had expected of myself when I was younger? The answers to both of those questions, quite simply, were no and no, and I knew (and hoped) that something had to change. Rather than looking forward to an upcoming trade show as a chance to break away from the normal routine and as an opportunity to catch up with colleagues and acquaintances, I dreaded the thought of going because I didn't want to spend my time looking at people that I did not want to be or become. When I did go, I felt as if I was parading past a bunch of caged animals and was deeply resentful of the fact that I too was one of them. If only for my own self-worth, it was time to move on.

I had the desire and plenty of reasons that were good enough for me to make the break. Now all I had to do was figure out how to do it, and put my talk into action. I came to an immediate realization that I had to maintain some semblance of normalcy until I finished putting my children through college. But I also realized that that time would be coming soon and that I needed to start preparing. Because of my preparation, I was able to make the break, literally spend two years on the road, and have a somewhat independent existence afterwards. The process required to achieve independence is what the balance of this book is about.

These were my trigger events in starting me to seek an alternative to the conventional work world. Yours will be different. You may be confronted with an illness or a family crisis that will force you to change. You may be faced with a job loss and say to yourself, *"If I don't make a change now, when will I?"* You might even have your house burn down, take the insurance settlement and just say, *"Screw it, I'm out of here."* Regardless of whatever has triggered your decision or desire, you will still need to go through the processes discussed in this book to help you understand if it is possible and how to go about it.

Your First Questions

*Photograph of Tiger Stadium; courtesy of Ballparks of Baseball;
www.ballparksofbaseball.com. "So near and yet so far!"*

"...these walls are funny. First you hate them,
then you get used to 'em. Enough time passes,
it gets so you depend on 'em. That's 'institutionalized'..."

from the prison movie **The Shawshank Redemption**

Your first question in starting the journey towards personal independence should be — have you been *institutionalized?* Have you become so familiar with your present existence that you cannot imagine a life for yourself outside of it? Are you living in a prison that you have built yourself?

The next time you hear someone state that the only opportunity open to them if they left their job would be to flip burgers, ask yourself if it is true, or have they been *institutionalized?* The same would apply when someone says that they cannot get health insurance; that they cannot retire without a million dollars in the bank; or that they need to replace X% (or X+%) of their current income to retire (or to make a semblance of a change). The reality is that you do not know the answers to these concerns until you do your own personal research. But if you do take these types of statements at face value without checking, then maybe you have been *institutionalized.*

Part of being *institutionalized* is taking every newspaper article or stock broker's newsletter on the difficulty or impossibility of retirement to heart. The general message today seems to be that one or two million dollars in the bank may not be enough for you to leave your job safely. This may or may not be true. Certainly, if your vision of being independent is to have a large income with a yacht and a house on a golf course in Boca Raton, one or two million dollars in the bank will definitely not cover your expenses. If your sights are pointed in a different direction there is a good chance that you may be able to do fine with much less. Continuing along the line of this thinking, perhaps you should be more skeptical when you hear someone giving financial and investment advice, and ask yourself what's in it for them. Part of what's in it for them may be for you to keep letting them manage your assets for your future. In that case, the last thing that they will want is for you to make your future now because then you will not need them anymore. Furthermore, if you do any financial research, you will find that most brokers and advisors typically do not do any better than the overall market. That's not to say that all advice is bad; it just means that you should be a bit more aware when making a decision on whose advice to take.

REDEFINING RULES

A major part in bringing change into your life will be your willingness to redefine the rules of work, independence, and "so-called" retirement. Redefining the rules applies to all aspects of what you expect from an independent existence. One aspect will probably include changing what to expect in obtaining a health insurance policy. Rather than assume or speculate that you cannot get insurance, investigate to see what is available. Rather than assume that once you leave work there will be no more work-related opportunities, recognize that many people change careers or return to positions similar to what they had before taking some time off. To say that you will only be able to flip burgers is not only demeaning to those who do flip burgers; it is also a short-changed assessment of yourself. As for needing so much in the bank and so much income to retire, you should recognize that your life has many financial thresholds that do not all magically converge at the age of 65. Your financial needs are what you spend. Spend more, you will need more; spend less, you will need less. As for having a fully funded retirement, you may not want to retire completely. You could consider a blend of activities that includes some income-producing enterprises that will carry you well beyond the arbitrary age of 65. You may end up deciding to un-retire and re-retire several times during the remainder of your life. **In short, it's not setting you up for retirement that is important; it is providing yourself with an array of skills and activities for a sustainable self-sufficient existence that is important!** An independent course starts with your acting independently, and a major part of acting independently is redefining how the rules apply to you.

ARE YOU A DOER?

Assuming that you have not been *institutionalized* and are willing to redefine rules where needed, you need to ask yourself — will you? If you are not a doer right now, what is it about the chance to live on the road that is going to change your non-doing ways? (On the other hand it could be that the reason that you have not been a doer is because you have not found anything compelling enough to prompt you into doing. So there may be an opportunity for those who are not yet doing.) If you are deferring projects or goals for when you are retired, why aren't you doing something about them right now? Can you absolutely guarantee that you will be here tomorrow? The time to be living and doing is right now regardless of your state of employment or lifestyle. Time keeps moving on no matter where you are or what you are engaged in.

For instance, you may have a personal interest in traveling around the country to visit every major league baseball park (if not, think of something else) when retired. If this is an important interest to you, why wait until then? You do not have to get to every ballpark in one summer. You can get to them over time as

What Do You Want Do?

If you are serious about seeking independence now may be a good time for you to start keeping a notebook to record your thoughts. You may want to start by thinking about what you would like to do in your life. Some questions that you might ask are:

- Are there things you have dreamed of doing?
- What are they?
- Are they realistic and possible?
- Have you done any of them?
- How long have you wanted to do them?
- Are you making plans to do them?
- If not, why?
- When will you do them?
- What's stopping you from doing them? (money, time, someone else, or you)

As you go through this process remember that there are no right or wrong answers. This is only an attempt to help you assess where you are right now and not source material to share with a therapy group.

your travels and schedule allow. You might as well start acting now because you do not know if your favorite ballpark will still be standing when you finally do retire, nor do you know if you will still be standing when you reach that time. Ask yourself, what is the point of spending the majority of your life in an existence that matters little to you, while anticipating what you will do in a "so-called" retirement?

Can you expect to make a life for yourself on the road if you are not making a life for yourself outside of work right now? For example, I had a conversation a couple of years ago with a man who was bemoaning never getting to Tiger Stadium in Detroit. He told me that when he was a little boy that he would tune in the radio by the side of his bed to catch a scratchy reception from an out of town station broadcasting a Detroit Tigers game and falling asleep to the voice of Ernie Harwell calling the game. From that moment on he dreamed of going to Tiger Stadium (or Briggs Stadium as it was called then). Over thirty-five years later he still dreamed of going to Tiger Stadium; and now it's too late. The Tigers now play in a new ballpark.

We are not talking about a man living in Malawi or even California. We are talking about someone living in central Pennsylvania only about eight hours by car from Tiger Stadium.

Certainly in thirty-five years he could have saved up the money for two or three tanks of gas, a night's lodging at a cheap motel, and the price of a ticket or two. He certainly had time to get up the nerve to tell his wife that we are (or I am) going to Detroit for the weekend. This was a very doable dream. **If doable dreams are important enough to you to bemoan, but are not worth the effort for you to make the commitment to do, do you really think anything will change if you choose the road?** If you are not going to become a doer, then you might as well learn how to let go and not waste time on something you have no intention of doing.

A friend of mine told me about a great time he had one afternoon canoeing on a slack water portion of the upper Connecticut River and then stopping by a store right on the river later that day to get some supplies. The man working the counter, who had lived beside the river all his life, told him that he had always wanted to go canoeing on the river but had never gotten around to it. Why? How can someone in good health and not indigent want to do something only five minutes away for years and not do it? Again, you have to be a doer to bring change into your life. Talk is cheap, and it is a waste of time if you are not going to act.

So before you entertain notions about changing your life you need to ask yourself if you really are going to do something about it.

"The fault, dear Brutus, is not in our stars;
But in ourselves, that we are underlings."

Julius Caesar — William Shakespeare

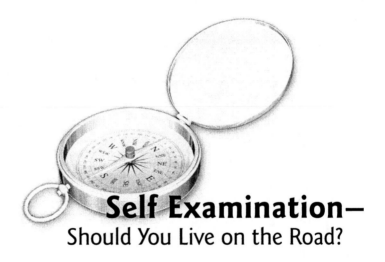

Self Examination—
Should You Live on the Road?

*Who knows where the winds
will let the leaf land?*

"The life which is unexamined is not worth living."

Socrates, from **The Apology** by Plato

I n keeping with the theme of doing something about your life, the first step in the process is to examine it. If you look at yourself, to paraphrase Henry David Thoreau, as *living a life of quiet desperation,* or are at a point of existential angst, or tired of perpetually being six weeks away from being fired, or yet again chasing another job with the same hollow promise of success, and long to do something different, the question you need to ask yourself is — what are you doing about it? Your choices are:

- To do nothing;

- To change your attitude towards what you are doing right now by acknowledging that this is what I do and engage in the moment. Or, as my dog Lucky, would tell you, "All walks are good; I don't know how long this walk is going to be, but I do know one thing, and that is that this is the best walk I have ever been on because this is the walk I am on right now;"

- Or, to make actual changes in your life.

I cannot say this enough — to bemoan and not act is a waste of your time, and a burden on those who have to listen to you. If you won't act, you should just let it go. But if you do act you may find that, with a few adjustments in lifestyle and attitude, you may be able to make serious and positive changes in your life.

I do not want to be so simple-minded as to say that all you need to do is to be positive, and poof, good things will happen for you. To make changes in your life requires thought and planning. It is certainly easier to make changes when times are good and the economy is rolling. But you do not have control over the state of the world, and sometimes you have to be willing to play the cards that have been dealt to you. But remember, just as good times do not last indefinitely, bad times, no matter how persistent, also do not remain. If you do hope to make a break from your current routine, now or in the future, the time to start planning for doing something about it is right now regardless of the day's headlines.

For Claudia and for me, the decision to leave a steady job to live on the road was not difficult. Others who are more career-minded or more concerned about being a pillar of the community than we may find it more difficult to make the same decisions as we did. I have no interest in selling anyone on making a decision that is not right for him or her. I am not interested in coming up with a list of things that you could do if you only quit your job. If you need my help on how to fill your day, you are not ready to make a change. I have no interest in trashing the work world as it offers for many their best means of making a living, an outlet for socialization, an opportunity for making a contribution, and a way to be connected to the world. I have no interest in trying to change the minds of those who believe that they will have to work forever and may never be able to retire or take time off. I am not looking for an argument with those who think it is wrong to live life unconventionally. What one believes or how one chooses to live their life is not my concern. My interest is only in showing others (and there have been many who have asked) how we were able to leave our jobs to live on the road and to take on a more independent existence.

WHAT'S REALLY EATING YOU?

First and foremost in making a decision to live on the road is to ask yourself—why are you interested in changing your life and should you change your life? Are you truly frustrated and miscast in your current role, or are you just angry at your boss? Are you really looking to change jobs rather than to change your life? The reality is that if you love your work and cannot imagine anything better, then there is no reason to consider a major change in your life. Your primary focus should be on figuring out how you can do what you are doing now for the rest of your life without *losing your relevance.* However, if you look at your life as a never-ending replay of the day before, then maybe it really is time to change.

The concept of doing work that you love for as long as you can deserves further examination. Maintaining your relevance and making sure that you are not hindering the advancement of others is important in ensuring that you can do what you love for as long as you can. No one wants to hear about how much better it was done in the old days. Ask yourself if there is anything more tiring than an often repeated war story of how it used to take a real tiger to get the job done back then. If or when you reach the point of telling those stories, you better take it as a signal to move on.

Maintaining your relevance or making a change is really all about mastering the two most important duties of your life—knowing both how to live and how to die. Living would be described as being engaged as best as you can in the present moment in order to make a contribution. Dying could then be described as knowing when to step back to where you came from, knowing that you gave it your best, and letting someone else have their chance to show what they can do. It is by knowing when to move on to something new that you can give yourself an opportunity to experience the exhilaration of a personal rebirth. Reincarnation is now.

A chance for personal rebirth is within reach because making the change to reinvent yourself may be one of the few decisions in your life that is completely under your control. How many of the events in your life were the result of drifting along and were out of your control, much like a leaf fluttering to the ground? Who knows where the winds will let the leaf land? Think about your life. Jobs or relationships may have taken you down one path with many twists and turns to where you ended up right now. Friends and family followed their own path, and there is a good chance that what you once had in common is now hard to recognize. Now may be the time to take charge.

Before getting too excited about change it is important to consider and understand, even for those who do not necessarily love their job, the extent that your work plays in your own personal identity and self-esteem. Is it your work that makes you feel like a player. Is it the reason that you get up in the morning? Is it how you identify yourself? Is it your role and advancement within an organization or a field that gives you a sense of importance? It is necessary for you to ask yourself these questions and to realize that there are no right or wrong answers to them. You need to ask them to help you understand this aspect of yourself. There is nothing wrong about wanting to have a role or being able to make a contribution—it is part of what makes us feel valuable and alive. Part of choosing independence will be to understand the role these items play in your life and how you can achieve a sense of them outside the structure of the conventional work world.

You certainly do not want to step into a situation where you suffer from a loss of identity caused

What Makes You Feel Valuable?

Again this may be a good time bring out your notebook and jot down some items regarding your self-identity.

- How do you identify yourself?
- What makes you feel like a player and important?
- How much of what makes you feel valuable is work related?
- How much of what makes you feel valuable is outside of work?
- Do you see yourself being able to make a contribution outside of work?

Again there are no right or wrong answers for these questions.

by changing from being a person of "importance" into being person of "nothingness." To avoid this you will want to clearly define to yourself what gives you a sense of "importance" and look to blend several activities in your new life that will allow you to achieve this. For instance, you may have decided that you want to become a craftsman of some sort and have made the conscious decision to take on a so-called "lesser" job to keep the lights burning while you master the craft. In this scenario it is the craft that defines your importance, and the ancillary activities are there to help you achieve your dream. Another approach is not to worry about "importance" and recognize that anything and everything you do is or can be important regardless of what it is. Hopefully, whatever path you choose will enable you to grow and to contribute in many ways. Ultimately, you would like to be proud of the change you have made rather than be in a situation where you would be embarrassed or humiliated if someone from your previous existence were to stumble upon you.

This brings us back to beginning of this section on why do you want to leave your present situation? It is easy to focus on what's wrong, but have you looked at what's right? Your challenge in bringing change to your life will be to give yourself a fresh start that reduces the items that are wrong without losing all of what's right. There are many compelling reasons for choosing independence. You just want to make sure that when you leave your present life you are doing it to embrace a new life for yourself. You want to be able to refer to yourself in the present tense (I am), rather than in the past tense (I was). When you do reference the past, it should be in the context of "I have done" rather "I used to be."

What's Right—What's Wrong In Your Situation?

This is a good time to start thinking about what's right and what's wrong in your present situation. You could even start by making two separate lists in your notebook. By doing so you will begin to identify what you want to eliminate or minimize and what you want to retain or incorporate in your new existence. Refining this list over time will start the process of preparing a blueprint of what your new life could and should be.

THE NEXT CONSIDERATION—"THE WORLD'S BEST—AND WORST—EXCUSE: THE FAMILY"

Your family status will have a great deal to say in what type of road experience or independence, if any, is available to you. If you have growing children, literally living on the road may not make any sense at all. Unless you are quite well off, there will be a serious financial commitment that will last until your kids complete their education that will most likely require your continued employment. More important than the financial aspect of raising children is the implied responsibility of providing a stable environment that may be difficult to achieve while on the road. An exception to this would be if your vision of the road and independence is of adopting a new lifestyle in reasonably stable surroundings.

Other family considerations that could limit your flexibility could include caretaking elderly parents or a family member with a severe illness, or even having a menagerie of pets. Although these situations may make literally living on the road impractical, they do not have to preclude you from bringing change in your life. Another family-related consideration could be that of the

What About Singles?

Because Claudia and I declared our independence together, much of this narrative has been presented from the perspective of a couple. It is also quite possible for a single person to want to make a break and to declare their independence. However, it is probably important for many single people to make sure that their independent life retains as much of their personal support infrastructure of friends, family and activities as practical. In that case it would not be a wise choice to break away completely from all socialization and drift alone. To that end a reduced workload or part-time status to provide time for other interests may be a sensible alternative to leaving a job completely.

One of our single friends has successfully made the switch from fulltime to part-time status and now wonders how she had enough time to work fulltime. She is currently evaluating relocation opportunities for when she completely leaves the work world. Her criteria for a new location, beyond the normal desirables, is that there is proximity to friends and the activities she likes. In that way she plans to retain a sufficient level of her infrastructure while making room for new activities.

role that your extended family expects of you, such as being "the" successful businessman, "the" lawyer, "the" city person, or even "the" town drunk. If you no longer want to play your expected role and just want to become a cowboy poet, you have to ask yourself whose life is it and who's in charge of this decision? You shouldn't have to freeze your life because of what someone else expects of you. As long as you are meeting your responsibilities, you shouldn't be made to feel guilty about your decisions. If someone else is inconvenienced, then that's their problem; not yours.

Again, for Claudia and for me, our family situation lent itself for allowing us to declare our independence. My children had completed their education and were reasonably launched into adulthood. We also had each other for support, and neither of us had a high socialization need that would make it difficult for us to leave our jobs.

SOCIALIZATION NEED

Some people thrive and are energized by being around other people. Others are quite content to be by themselves and find too much socialization to be exhausting. A high need for socialization is not a show stopper for choosing independence. It is, however, an influence on what type of independent lifestyle and activities are best suited for you. If you are uncertain about your need for socialization and other personality drivers in your life, you can take a Myers-Briggs Type Indicator test. (Information on taking a test may available from your Human Resources department at work. If not, there is plenty of information on the Internet.)

The test evaluates four basic personality factors including extroversion versus introversion. The Indicator's definition of extroversion relates to whether you obtain energy from an outer world of people; while its definition of introversion relates to whether you obtain energy from an inner world of ideas. The test indicates whether you are an 'E' (extrovert) or an 'I' (introvert) and to what degree. Certainly if you are a strong 'E' you may want to think twice before abandoning civilization and moving to a deserted island; however, if you are a strong 'I', a deserted island may be just the revitalizing experience that you have been seeking.

CONCLUSION

The more you know about yourself, the easier it will be for you to understand whether you can make a break from your current routine. If it turns out that you made a bad decision in choosing change, it will not be the end of the world. You can always re-enter the work world and look at your time on the road as the same as you would look upon a poor job choice. If you do decide to re-enter the workforce, the quality of the jobs available to you will be more of a factor of the current state of the economy rather than the fact that you tried out something different (read "temporarily dropped out"). More than likely, people that you will talk to about employment will find your time off from work as something of interest and will not hold it against you. There is a very good likelihood that a potential employer will appreciate your ability and willingness to set a goal and to make the necessary commitment to achieve it.

I certainly know that in my situation most of the people I have done contract work for after declaring my independence have looked upon my actions as a positive. In one case while I was at a company function, the person in charge of the division I was helping out kept telling everyone how I walked the entire Appalachian Trail and then rode my bike from Chicago to Washington, DC. Later that evening his boss came up to me to say that it was good to have people around who know how to make things happen. Doing something different than a "career" will not be a black mark on your permanent record that will follow you for the rest of your life.

Hitting the Road—
Understanding What You Want to Do

*The road always leading one beyond
the horizon. Photograph by the author.*

Alexander Throckmorton

In youth my wings were strong and tireless,
But I did not know the mountains
In age I knew the mountains
But my weary wings could not follow my vision —
Genius is wisdom and youth.

from Spoon River Anthology *—* by Edgar Lee Masters

I f you have cleared the first hurdle of deciding whether you should go on the road, your next step should be to think about what you would like to accomplish on the road. Or in keeping with the spirit of the opening quote, it would be using your wisdom to pursue your vision. Understanding what you want to accomplish on the road is the most important aspect of your planning. (In fact, if what you want to do is compelling enough you will probably figure out a way to make the rest of the necessary actions fall in place.) It is important to know what you want to accomplish, because we all most likely have anecdotal evidence and perhaps personal knowledge of people who were let go from their jobs or left their jobs without any real plan and ended up bored out of their minds and with diminished life force. You do not want to end up feeling like you are sitting on the bench, irrelevant, and out of the action. Nor, do you want to be looking at an airplane flying overhead and think that you should be on it going somewhere to do something important. It is important "to be" wherever you are, and I would hope that you use your opportunity for independence to do more and more rather than less and less. If you use your gift of time to wander around aimlessly, I would fear that you could look back at your time on the road as a squandered opportunity. For me, I looked at my time on the road as a series of missions to fulfill personal dreams, interests, and commitments. If you are not a self-starter, leaving the structure of the regular work world may not be best for you.

So why do you want to go on the road and what are you going to do? I can't answer that, only you can. As I said earlier, if you need me to come up with a list of things to do for you, you are not ready to go on the road. Again, if you have not made a life for yourself outside of work or family, are you going to make a life for yourself on the road? I can share with you some of the thought processes I went through, and perhaps that can help you in your planning. First off, the work world was okay for me but it was not my overriding passion. It was a way that I knew how to make enough money to meet my financial responsibilities. My passions were and continue to be the many interests and curiosities that I have had all my life. For as long as I can remember my favorite things to do have been checking things out, prowling around, and sending away. One of the thrills of my life was to actually make a pilgrimage to Battle Creek, Michigan to see the Kellogg's cereal factory where I had sent away so many box tops.

I found it difficult to pursue my personal interests to the extent that I wanted while still fully engaged in the work world. Because of that, I resolved from the moment I stepped into my first "corporate" job that I would adopt a more independent lifestyle as soon as I could. As I said in the opening, my only problem was that I did not know how to break away. Finally when I focused myself, I decided to make the break when my kids completed college.

LIFE PHASES OR QUARTERS

I look at my time of being fully engaged in the work world as one phase of my life and what I am doing now as a different phase. As you continue your research in changing your life, you may run across an Asian concept of looking at your life in "quarters." The "quarters" of your life are: childhood/youth (growing up and going to school); the early productive years (developing your career and child rearing); the later productive years (for processing life and contributing in other ways); and the older less energetic years (to pass along wisdom). This contrasted to the more conventional approach of three life phases: youth, the productive years and retirement. (In some Asian countries it is in the third quarter that many people go to a monastery and become a Buddhist monk.) The "quarters" of your life do not have to be of equal duration and will vary depending on your personal circumstances. The "quarters" approach does, however, eliminate the sharp cleavage between the productive years and retirement. Having such a sharp break between work and retirement raises a legitimate concern about losing one's purpose in life and ignores the possibility that one's productive years could be (and perhaps should be) as long as one has the energy and health to make a contribution. Can a society really afford not to seek and welcome the contribution from all of those who are able?

Additionally, as I mentioned earlier, we do not know if we will get to be old or how we will get old. We may have robust health into our 80's, or we may drop dead unexpectedly before we are 60. We just do not know. Because of that, one should make their mark when they can and not wait for an arbitrary age for when they are allowed to strike out on their own. Every day is a gift that should be lived to its fullest. Using freed-up time to process what you have learned in life while you still have the energy may lead to a better understanding of life.

OUR PLANNING PROCESS

Claudia and I met later in our lives, and from that moment on we began planning our independence and were able to achieve it three years later. We were ready for independence and at the point in life to pull it off. In my case, I am not sure if I have ever been part of any group where I really felt that I belonged. I have always been restless and wanting to step out into a world of adventure. And as for Claudia, she is the only person I know other than myself, who has read all of Richard Halliburton's 1930s era adventure books. (If you are not familiar with Richard Halliburton, go to your local library and check out some of his adventures.) In short, we were both open to something new.

As for our planning, the first thing we did was to start identifying things that we would like to do. From that process we developed a short list of some major activities and built around them. We had always wanted to learn how other people in the world live. We investigated the Peace Corps and other international opportunities. We eventually decided against the Peace Corps because of the length of the application process and the uncertainty of when we could start. We kept looking and finally decided upon volunteering at an economic development center in a small village in the Philippines operated by some friends of ours that Claudia met at her church.

We found from our investigations that international and domestic service opportunities are abundant. You can find them by checking out religious organizations, activist organizations, NGOs (Non-Governmental Organizations) and organizations such as Habitat for Humanity. Many opportunities are volunteer projects that are structured around a typical one to two-week vacation period. For instance, if you like hiking, the American Hiking Society has many trail-building vacations.

In considering any volunteer opportunity, you need to find out if you will be doing scut work that could be done by anyone, with the primary purpose of keeping you busy, out of the way, out of mischief, and making you "feel" like you are making a contribution, or if you will actually be contributing your skills to make a difference. If you want something more than a feel-good opportunity, you may have to dig harder. If you can make a longer (over one year) time commitment, there are the Peace Corps and many teaching and health care opportunities. Because these opportunities are always changing, I would start the search through your personal network of friends and affiliations. Many churches are involved in sponsoring overseas educational and developmental centers that do not involve religious work or require you to be a missionary.

In our situation, we approached our friends with the economic development center in the Philippines to see if there was anything we could do to be of value. They then came up with a list of tasks that they thought we could accomplish. They also arranged for us to stay at the center and for one of the local staff to prepare meals for us at a very reasonable fee. The cost was so reasonable that our inflow of funds from our financial planning efforts was much greater than our outflow of funds while staying in Asia. To complement our stay in the Philippines we tacked on a one-month trip to China. All together we planned for three months in Asia.

With three months of our new lifestyle accounted for, we set our sights on other projects. In addition to an overseas project, we were also interested in living in simplicity, having a quiet time for a contemplative experience, immersing ourselves in nature, being physically challenged, and having an opportunity for adventure. Through a series of coincidences, we discovered the Appalachian Trail and added a six-month end-to-end thru-hike of the 2160-mile trail to our list of things to accomplish. (If you are interested in hiking the Appalachian Trail, or going on a long-distance hike, there are many books on the subject including one I wrote, **Long Distance Hiking on the Appalachian Trail for the Older Adventurer.**)

With two major projects in place, we knew we would pretty much spend the first year of our new life literally on the road. Even though we had many more items on our list, we did not want to micromanage our lives too far out into the future. We wanted to see how events would unfold to allow for flexibility. What we had were lists of supplemental activities and goals that could be fit around a major activity or could be saved for a later time. Some of them, such as running in a marathon and plotting out (and riding on) a bike trail from Chicago to Washington, D.C. using abandoned canal and rail right-of-ways as much as possible, had been on my wish list since high school. Claudia added to the list a very personal activity of following U.S. Highway 41 from end to end. U.S. Highway 41 runs south from the northern tip of Michigan's Upper Peninsula through Milwaukee, Chicago, Nashville, Atlanta and Tampa to its endpoint in Miami, Florida. Much of Claudia's life had revolved around U.S. 41 (she had grown up in Nashville, vacationed as a kid in Florida, lived with her first husband in the Upper Peninsula of Michigan, and ended up in Chicago), and she wanted to follow it in its entirety.

Our list contained many more items than those mentioned, and rather than shrinking, our list continues to grow. To complement the list of activities, we had our lists of interests, events, and places that we could check out as time and chance allowed. For us, those items included Native American culture, archaeology, solar eclipses, natural hot springs, regional differences, regional street food, baseball games, wildlife, scenic wonders, Civil War sites, hikes, and many many more. Because there were so many things that I have always wanted to check out, I had long kept a database of items of interest to me. The database was originally on index cards and has now migrated to a personal computer. Whenever something caught my attention, it went into the database. Now whenever I plan to go to an area, I can look into the database to see if there is something that I should be checking out.

YOUR PLANNING PROCESS

Our interests may seem inane and should be irrelevant to you. What is important is that you structure your time around what is meaningful to you. What I hope you obtain from this discussion is the value of having an iterative process of categorizing potential projects and having some major projects (in our case going to Asia and hiking the Appalachian Trail) to build around. With some major projects in place, you can then determine how to fit in some smaller activities and goals. The final step would be to use your interests and events to round out what you are doing. It is not necessary to micromanage your time on the road. With a multi-level approach you can rearrange your plans as conditions warrant, much like a football quarterback calling an audible when seeing something he did not like about the defensive line-up.

As it turns out, we had enough initial activities to keep us literally on the road for two years. During that time we did not have a permanent home and did not do any "work" related activities. We then shifted our on the road experience into a more metaphorical phase that we are still in—engaging in a new lifestyle with some work, living in a new location, and pursuing a completely different array of interests. We do see in the not too distant future more forays into extended periods of being away from home. The important lesson is that by knowing what we wanted to accomplish and continue to want to accomplish, we have not run out of things to do and look forward to engaging in many more activities. Also in seven plus years we have not felt compelled to return to the regular work world on a fulltime or permanent basis.

One person I know in his later fifties, who at the time of this writing is considering leaving his job within the year, is right now in the process of categorizing what he would like to accomplish with his newfound freedom. He is toying around with two major activities. One is to spend an entire winter in an isolated cabin in Alaska and the other is to spend several months living at and working out daily in a martial arts dojo. With this head start on what he would like to do, he can now go the next step of doing his homework to turn these dreams into reality.

A very close friend of mine has just completed the shift to an independent life. He is just short of fifty. In his case, he was faced with complications from diabetes and knew he had to make a change to preserve what health he had left. He and his wife had always wanted a farm and were able to find a small one they could afford in southern Missouri. With the proceeds of selling their house in a major metropolitan area and a small amount of disability income because of the diabetes, they have been able to afford making the switch from the world of commerce to independence. In the process of bringing the farm back into shape, he has found time for contemplation and has engaged in enough physical activity to keep his blood sugar and health in check. He is now metaphorically, *on the road*. His only question now is — why did he wait so long?

What you do not want is to end up like a business acquaintance of mine. When he was in his late fifties, the large corporation he was working for downsized. He was offered a severance package that most people could only dream about — immediate full retirement with full medical coverage. When he hemmed and hawed about the offer, his boss told him, *"If you don't take this offer, I'll fire you because I don't want anyone that stupid working for me."* Six months later he was back working at another job. When I saw him at the new job, I asked him why, and he told me that he was tired of going to the shopping mall with his wife and had nothing else better to do. Even if you have never thought about being independent, you would be well served to have an idea of what you would do with the gift of time; in today's business environment, it just might be thrust upon you.

YOUR PARTNER'S ROLE

As the above example illustrates, it is important to consider the role of your partner, if you have one, in your new and independent life. Whether your partner currently stays at home or works out of the house, nothing will necessarily change for him or her just because you are no longer leaving the house to go to work. If it is not practical or possible for the two of you to become independent or to embrace change together, it is important that the two of you reach an understanding.

If you will now be based at home, it is important that you do not get in the way of your partner's normal routine. And on the other hand, your partner needs to recognize that just because you are at home you are not necessarily doing nothing and available to run errands at their beck and call. This is especially true if you are working on a home-based enterprise or project. A pattern of mutual respect and understanding of each other's boundaries and responsibilities is necessary for your experiment in independence to work. Otherwise, you may be anxiously running back to work after being dragged in and out of shopping malls for six months.

If your vision and plans for independence call for some out-of-the-house or on-the-road type projects that your partner will not be able to participate in, it is again important to reach an understanding. It is important that your plans do not neglect your responsibilities to each other. It would also be beneficial that both of you work together in developing both of your plans. In that way you can make sure that there is time for projects that you will do on your own and for those projects that you will do together. It is important to take your partner into consideration because your experiment (or partnership) could be short lived if your partner believes that you are having all the fun while he or she is left holding the bag. Your plans for independence will work for you only if they work for both of you.

PLAN NOW

Again, I cannot say it enough—the time for planning for your future is now; not just your finances but also what you would like to achieve. Nothing in life is guaranteed—your job could disappear, your health could deteriorate, the trend of world events could take a direction not to your liking, and who knows? The more you can develop outside of your work in the form of income sources, involvements, interests and goals, the more you will get out of your independence whether you eagerly seek it or have it dumped in your lap. There can be a life outside of what you currently know, and for many it has proven to be good.

"For the mistake is thinking that that quantity of experience depends on the circumstances of our life when it depends solely on us. . . . To two men living the same number of years, the world always provides the same sum of experiences. It is up to us to be conscious of them. Being aware of one's life, one's revolt, one's freedom, and to the maximum, is living, and to the maximum."

The Myth of Sisyphus — **Albert Camus**

Financial Planning—
Can You Afford to Go on the Road?

Photograph of Shaker Meeting House, Mt. Lebanon Shaker Village, New York; courtesy of Jerry Brewington.

"Simple Gifts"

'Tis the gift to be simple,
'Tis the gift to be free,
'Tis a gift to come down
Where we ought to be.
And when we find ourselves
In the place just right
Twill be in the valley
Of love and delight.

19th century Shaker tune

If you have cleared the first hurdle of determining that living on the road is right for you and have an understanding of what you want to accomplish, the next step is to consider the financial planning aspects of leaving a steady job. Or, can you afford to be *in the place just right?* Affordability will vary depending upon personal circumstances. Some of you may be wealthy and have no financial concerns. Others of you may have pensions or other income source(s) that will fully replace your current income right now. You may even have full medical coverage. Then there will be others of you who will have no guaranteed immediate income or guaranteed health coverage. If that is the case, your challenge will be to find replacements outside of a regular job.

Claudia and I fit into that last category. We were not wealthy; and because we left our jobs voluntarily, we did not have a severance or guaranteed health coverage beyond the normal COBRA period. Furthermore it would be a long time before we would be qualified to receive Social Security or pension benefits. We had to make provisions to provide for our income and to pay for our health coverage in our independent lifestyle. In short, proper financial planning was crucial for us.

If you are somewhat conventional and not a total dropout, money will be an important consideration in your decision-making. But before leaving the topic of dropouts, please keep in mind that there are lots of people who have never even bothered to enter the regular work world who are doing just fine. They have been content with a different standard of living while chasing their pursuits. But for those with financial concerns (most of us) your financial planning can be looked upon as putting the legs on a three-legged stool. They are:

- having enough funds for an adequate "traditional" retirement,

- buying health insurance,

- and finding sources of current income.

I am not a financial planning expert and don't expect this book to be a financial planning guide or a roadmap to certain wealth. Go to any bookstore, and you will find hundreds of financial planning guides. Check out the Internet, and you will see that every search engine, every financial service provider, and every major media outlet has a personal financial planning section. Please note that whatever you read will have a point of view and you will have to decide how their advice applies to you. I'll just discuss briefly items to consider in your planning.

RETIREMENT

The term retirement is used here only to acknowledge the need to have adequate funds for your later years. It is not used here as an endorsement of a lifestyle or as a need to replace a certain percentage of your current income. Hopefully, in moving on to the road, you will be taking on interests and activities that will keep you engaged in life for as long as your health and energy allow.

The first step in determining if you have funds for an adequate retirement is to calculate/estimate what you think you will have available to you at the traditional retirement age of 65. Although 65 is an arbitrary age, it is a good benchmark for your planning purposes in making sure that you have your later years covered. Your retirement income sources will come from Social Security, pension(s) that you are qualified for, and personal financial resources (401Ks, IRAs, investments, and savings). Your house and other non-financial assets may or may not be a factor in your post-65 income.

The future viability of Social Security has

Reverse Mortgage

If you are 62 or older you can look into the suitability of a reverse mortgage as a way of tapping into your home's equity to contribute to your cash flow. A reverse mortgage allows you to access your home's equity without selling it. Instead of paying down a loan as with a normal mortgage, you will be building up a loan balance as you access the equity. As long as you live in the home you will not have to pay back the loan. Information on reverse mortgages is available from banks, AARP, and on the Internet. In making a decision on using a reverse mortgage you will have to consider the impact of the local real estate market on your home's value, the cost of interest, and whether you really want to stay in the house. In other words, do your homework before signing on the dotted line.

If you are not close to the age of 62, I would be reluctant to put a reverse mortgage on your radar scope for planning purposes. Too much can change between now and then in the real estate market. Housing values could change, interest rates could change, and legislation could change the rules. You may want to look at whatever your house can provide for the post-65 years as a bonus.

If you have substantial equity in your home and are well under 62, you can always look into a home equity loan as a means to tap into the home's value. Again you will have to do the same homework and make the same decisions as you would with any other loan. A loan is a loan regardless of how you secure it or when you have to pay it back.

been a major discussion topic for several years. According to the Social Security Administration, if nothing is changed, Social Security will begin paying out more than it collects within fourteen years (2018). Again if nothing is done and the projections are correct, the Social Security Trust Fund will be exhausted by 2042. The general aging of the population does add some credibility to this concern. If the pessimists are correct, the personal benefit statements provided by Social Security on what you can expect to receive may not represent what you will actually get. As the ratio of workers to retirees shifts there is a possibility that benefits could be cut. It is unlikely that they will completely disappear; however, for your planning purposes, you can consider underweighting the contribution of Social Security to your post-65 income.

In considering pensions, remember that not all companies provide them. It is estimated that only 20% of private employees are covered by a defined benefit plan (pension). If your employer is one of those who provides a defined benefit plan, you may have to be employed there for a minimum of five years before you are vested (qualified to receive benefits) in their plan. The amount you will receive will be dependant upon your length of service and your income. Because plans vary you will want to check with your current employer and former employers to see if you are qualified to receive a pension. If you are qualified, you will want to ask them what you will receive in monthly income at the age of 65 based upon your current level of service if you were to leave work right now. Unless you have close to 20 years of service, it is unlikely that you will come close to replacing a significant percentage of your present income. However, as an independent person you should not be expecting to obtain income from only one source. You should look upon what you do receive as a bonus and that much less that you have to worry about.

Because pensions and similar financial incentives are tied to years of service, it is important to find out from your employer if there are any critical thresholds approaching that will have an impact on your becoming vested in a plan or becoming eligible to receive a significant amount of money. You do not want to do anything stupid like leave a job six months before you would be vested in a pension plan or in your employer's matching contribution to a 401(k) program. The same consideration of critical dates would apply to commissions or bonuses if you are on an incentive compensation plan.

As for your personal resources, you will want to conservatively estimate what they will be worth at the age of 65. As the volatility in the stock market has shown in the past few years, it is best to err on the side of caution. You can easily use a spreadsheet program to make this estimate, or use a financial calculator from a financial service provider's Internet site. The purpose of this drill is to predict what the value of your financial assets will be at the age of 65. Your determination would factor in what you have now, what you plan to add, what you expect to return annually, and what you anticipate inflation to be. No matter what technique you use, it will still only be an estimate. An estimate is sufficient for now as you are only trying to see if you are comfortable with how much you have set aside to date. The reality is that if you really do not want to make the break you will come up with several reasons why the numbers do not work—what if inflation takes off, what if the stock market tanks, what if, what if, what if? On the other hand if you do want to make the break, you will bend over backwards to make the numbers work. You just do not want to bend so far over that you start fooling yourself.

Your total age 65 retirement income estimate would then be based upon the total of:

- Social Security,

- Pensions,

- And what you can comfortably withdraw from your personal resources each year.

Building Your Retirement Assets

Because of the importance of building retirement assets, it is worthwhile to look at the effectiveness of your job history in accomplishing this. Are you accumulating assets? Are you at least contributing an amount equal to your employer's match in your company's 401(k) program? Are you staying long enough at the company to become vested in their pension (if available) or in their matching contribution to your 401(k)? Are you participating in company stock purchase programs (if available)? Or, are you chasing pipe dreams?

In my pre-independence industry IT (Information Technology), many people I knew were lured by the dream (usually from start-up companies) of a hot product that would take over the world overnight and stock options that would make them fabulously wealthy when the company was taken public. In some very isolated cases, some people I knew actually did hit a grand slam home run and came out as winners. Unfortunately, the vast majority came out with a big fat zero. They then oftentimes went on to another fabulous promise with the same empty result. Some have repeated the process six or seven times over a ten or twelve year period. Ask yourself, who is more likely to accumulate adequate retirement assets—someone who went to work for six or seven start-up companies that went nowhere over a twelve year period, or someone who stayed long enough at one or two jobs in that same ten or twelve year period to become vested in their company's pension or matching contribution to their 401k?

Withdrawing Funds from Your Personal Assets

When it comes time to actually cash in on your financial assets to round out your post-65 income, you will need to determine how much you can withdraw annually. You will have to balance having enough to get by on and not outliving your money. Generally a withdrawal amount of four or five percent a year is considered reasonable. Conservatively managed assets should provide a combined interest, dividend and appreciation return in that range. An asset mix providing that level of return, while not high risk, does require that you take on more risk than putting it into a passbook savings account earning less than 1% a year. You will need to do your homework to determine how best to manage your different sources of income to meet your requirements.

If you are comfortable with your potential post-65 income, it becomes much easier to make the decision to make a major lifestyle change. If you have enough money set aside for age 65, you will have the added benefit of reducing your current expenses by the amount that you no longer need to set aside for age 65. If you do make a change in your lifestyle, you will need to manage your money carefully. It is your future and "nest egg" that you are now stewarding. If your post-65 funds, however, are not sufficient, you at least have a heads-up on what you need to accumulate before you can become independent.

Even if you are not comfortable with your potential post-65 income, it does not mean that you cannot change your lifestyle. It only means that at some time you will need to make a conscientious effort to earn enough money for age 65 and beyond. It could also mean that you will need to return to a regular job after you accomplish your initial goals on the road. Or, you may even want to look at your time on the road as an opportunity to develop skills for a new career or enterprise that you could commit yourself to well beyond the age of 65.

HEALTH INSURANCE

Heath insurance is usually a major bugaboo in most peoples' mind when they think about leaving the regular work world. This is for good reason because without a job you will now be responsible for taking on a major and uncertain expense that you may not currently see if you are in a group medical plan. Your situation will become the same as a self-employed person or small businessman. Part of your success in leaving a regular job will be in your ability to change your mindset from that of an employee to that of an entrepreneur or small businessman. Your new lifestyle will become your new business.

The world of health care and health insurance is a moving target. What applies today may not apply tomorrow. Right now, when you leave your job, you will have the option of buying health insurance through your employer at your employer's cost for 9–18 months, depending upon the size of your employer, under your COBRA rights. When the COBRA period expires you will be on your own regarding health insurance. Until there is a change in public policy, you will most likely find health insurance to be very expensive to buy on your own. In our case we found a high-deductible major medical policy to be the most economical way of protecting ourselves and our resources from catastrophic illness. These policies, too, are not cheap and will vary in cost depending upon your age, location, and medical history. A major medical policy means that instead of making a modest co-payment, you will now be paying for routine medical visits out of pocket in addition to the cost of the insurance policy. It also means that when you do have a major illness you will have to cover the cost of a substantial deductible before the coverage kicks in.

Recent legislation now allows you to open a Health Savings Account (HSA) if you have a high deductible insurance policy. The HSA allows you to shelter income from taxation and to use funds in the account to pay for medical expenses. It is a back-handed way of making more of your medical expenses tax deductible and takes a small amount of the sting out of the cost of health insurance. At the time of this writing, HSAs are very new and are mainly being offered by insurance companies in conjunction with health insurance policies.

The fact that you will find health insurance to be expensive does not mean that you have no other choice but to hang on to your job in order to go to the doctor. It only means that health insurance and medical costs are expense items that you will have to take into consideration in your budgeting. Accepting the cost of medical care may be easier to swallow if you consider that in becoming independent you could be eliminating many of your work related expenses such as commuting, business clothes, eating lunch out everyday, and office socialization. If you are truly concerned about medical coverage and still want to take time off to hit the road, you can think in terms of returning to a regular job before the COBRA period expires. You may even want to look at a half-time job that provides some form of health insurance coverage.

If you are hoping to make your change permanent and do not expect to be back in a group medical policy after the COBRA period expires, you should consider making the jump to a major medical policy or alternative immediately. If your health changes during the COBRA period, it may be harder or more expensive to obtain coverage when the period expires. Insurance companies do not want to expose themselves to an obvious risk, and if you have a serious condition, you may have to rely upon a state-sponsored risk pool to obtain coverage. Before turning in

Canadian Prescription Option

If you are a U.S. citizen and have a chronic condition that requires prescription medication, you can usually save a significant amount of money by buying your medication outside of the country. As mentioned in the narrative (see next page) there are many interests opposed to U.S. citizens buying prescription drugs from Canada or other countries; therefore, the future viability of this option is up the air. At the time of this writing there are many Canadian pharmacies that can be accessed over the Internet. Web sites include www.canadarx.net, www.canadadrugs.com, and many others. They can be found by doing a search on the Internet.

The sources generally work as follows:

- The first step is to access the Canadian pharmacy through the Internet with their web address (see above).
- Once you are at their web site you can enter the name of your medication to determine its availability and to receive a price quote. In that way you can determine if there is enough savings to warrant proceeding. Some of the sites will quote in Canadian dollars. This will require that you to perform a quick currency conversion to determine the exact amount of the savings.
- If you decide to proceed, you will then need to fax your prescription to the pharmacy (for this you will need your physician's cooperation) and provide them a credit card number for charging your purchase. The instructions on doing this can be found on the pharmacy's web site.
- The pharmacy will then ship you the medication and charge your credit card. Your credit card company will automatically perform any necessary currency conversion. Credit card companies are very good about providing the best available currency conversion rate.

With those steps you can now save money on your prescription drugs.

your notice to your employer, you should talk to some insurance companies about your insurability and options available to you.

Because of the expense of medical care, you will want to look for any angle you can to reduce your exposure. You will want to check out associations and groups that you can possibly join for their medical plans. You could look into what coverage is available through a college and become a part-time student. If you have expensive prescription drugs, you will definitely want to check out buying your drugs in Canada or Mexico. Claudia and I have saved almost $1,000 a year by buying prescriptions in Canada. Others I know are saving more. Keep in mind that there are people in the pharmaceutical industry who are trying to shut the window on obtaining medications from out of the country, and the Canadian option may no longer be available by the time you read this book.

The bottom line is that before you throw your hands up in the air and surrender on the issue of health insurance, do your homework. Find out the alternatives available to you and see how they fit in your overall budget. Once you know the choices, you can then make a decision.

Current Income

The easiest source of current income for people without a regular job is to have money. This is great, but for the rest of us it is necessary to have income sources outside of a steady job to be able to leave that steady job. The first step in making a lifestyle change is to determine how much you can simplify your life. As I mentioned in the beginning, I believe that, unless you are shifting to a new lifestyle with adequate income, it is helpful for your children to be launched into the adult world before considering a significant lifestyle change. Once your kids are out of the house, you will find a dramatic reduction in your expenses as long as you resist the temptation to intervene financially in their lives. When you are in a position of no longer caring for children, no longer saving for retirement, and of having simplified your life, you will find that you can now live on significantly less money than before. If you are planning to sell your house to live on the road as Claudia and I did, you will have made another major reduction in expenses. The more you can eliminate on the expense side, the less you will need to produce on the income side of the ledger.

If you do not know where to start simplifying your expenses, you can begin by examining how you are spending your money right now. You will be surprised, if not shocked, at how much the

What Is Simplification?

This book uses the term "simplification" in the context of managing your lifestyle to reduce or limit how much money you need to bring in to meet your financial obligations. Simplification is merely a means to provide you the flexibility to do things beyond worrying about how to make a living. Simplification can come through active intervention, or by passively waiting for an obligation to end. In our case we actively simplified through the selling of our house, and passively simplified when my children completed college. Later in our journey when we purchased a new house, we spent less than half of what we spent prior to declaring our independence.

There is also, if you will, a voluntary simplification movement that looks at ways to improve the overall quality of life through reduced consumption. In many cases, people have almost turned simplification into a game to find imaginative ways to save money. There are many newspaper columns, web sites and books devoted to simplification and ways to save money.

overhead of life (utilities, upkeep, cell phones, cable, alarm service, lawn service, Internet service, business services, subscriptions, storage, insurance and others) adds up. Once you know where your money goes you can identify where cuts, if any, can be made. You may discover many simplification opportunities, or you may discover that there are way too many obligations at the present moment to declare your independence now. If you do have obligations and do eventually want to become independent, you should have enough information after this examination to determine how, when, or if you can reduce those obligations to make a change.

If you determine that there is nothing that you want to reduce or eliminate, you have at least made the decision that protecting the status quo and your present lifestyle is more important to you than making a change. If that is your decision, then that's okay. You should just not go around bemoaning your situation after you have clearly made a decision. You should accept your decision as being the right choice for you.

If you do want to change, it is important to recognize that a significant part of the reason that it is difficult for people to become independent is that as a society we have increased and continue to increase the size our own personal economic footprint — compare the size and expense of automobiles, homes, personal furnishings, and other items to their equivalent of a generation or two ago. The ever increasing demands of our consumption-driven economy are continuously raising what is expected from us financially. Every day there seem to be new products and services enticing us to spend our money. Some may be real improvements, while others are truly indulgent or frivolous.

For example with our society's obsession on appearance, it may come to the point where we will all be expected to have regular Botox injections and teeth whitening treatments just to be presentable. God knows you don't want to look as old as you feel. Even if you believe that having a poison injected into your face as being ridiculous and the resulting "look" to be artificial, you may not have much of a choice in the matter if the "look" becomes the expected or the norm in certain professions after a certain age. It is this subtle persuasion that places an ever continuing pressure on our pocketbooks.

If you want to be independent, you'll have to stand up to the tastemakers and trend setters of the world, and say, "*Screw you. I don't care about your style. I don't care about what you expect of me. I care about my own personal freedom.*" At the same time you also have to recognize that no one is forcing you to spend your money. It is you who is pulling out the credit card to adhere to someone else's standards. You do have free will, and ultimately you are responsible for the state of your pocketbook. If you can reduce your economic footprint you will reduce your income requirements. By doing so you could be on the way to setting up a sustainable self-sufficient existence. Recognizing your ability to manage the size of your economic footprint is the first step towards financial independence, especially if you do not have substantial financial resources.

For the income side of the ledger, each person will have to find their own sources. These sources could be a military pension, severance package, investment real estate, a seasonal business, hobby business, investment strategies, savings, temporary or seasonal employment, contract work, withdrawing funds from your retirement accounts, disability payments, hustle, and/or other enterprises. In essence, you may end up managing a portfolio of income producing activities. If you intend to return to regular employment after being on the road, your savings and simplified lifestyle may be adequate for carrying you through a limited period of time. The more you would like to make your change permanent, the more important it is for you to develop other sources of income. The closer you can come to generating income

What Is The Size of Your Personal Economic Footprint?

You may complain, or hear from friends, that it now takes two incomes to support a household, whereas in a previous generation only one income was required to do the job. This could be true, but before buying into that argument you can examine your own economic footprint to determine if the equivalent of two incomes is a necessity. If it does take two incomes, you can find out if it is because one or both of you does not make enough money, or if you have expanded your economic footprint. You can begin your study by answering the following:

- What are your expenses?
- What are you spending on luxuries?
- How big is your house?
- How big is your car?
- How expensive are your vacations?
- Are they more than you can afford?
- How much debt are you carrying?
- Are the items above (your economic footprint) larger than you expected?
- Does it seem excessive?
- Is it growing?
- If it is excessive or growing, is it contributing to your need for extra income?
- Is this really what you want?
- Is this really improving the quality of your life?
- Would you like to change your economic footprint?
- Can you change it?
- Will you change it?

outside of a regular job greater than or equal to your expenses, the longer you can maintain your independence. Having a diverse portfolio of financial activities is your best protection against any changes in the economy, reductions in Social Security benefits or other surprises/disasters that may occur. **The key to maintaining an independent life is managing "the gap" between your expected income and expenses.** Or, by creating a self-sufficient existence for yourself by following the precept of the late ecologist Garrett Hardin of balancing usage with carrying capacity.

"The maximum is not the optimum"

Garrett Hardin

Opportunities for Income

There are job opportunities everywhere including temporary and seasonal employment for those nomads literally on the road. For many it is a major part of their *on the road* experience. These jobs can be found in national parks, ski resorts, or wherever there is a seasonal spike in usage. These jobs tend to be low paying and should only be looked upon as an opportunity to pick up some walking around money while spending time at a place that is special to you. When I was hiking the Appalachian Trail, I met a couple in their 50's who were living on the road. Their base income came from some rental property in their home town. While traveling around the country, they had spent the previous fall after the summer help went back to school working the front desk at one of the lodges in Yellowstone National Park. The job gave them a free place to stay, some walking around money, and the opportunity to be at the park for two months. When the lodge closed down for the winter, they then moved their act south to Everglades National Park in Florida where they were volunteers.

In return they received a free place to stay and a small stipend. When I met them, they were spending the summer on the Appalachian Trail patrolling a section of the trail as ridge runners again for a small stipend. Because they like to hike and meet people, they had found a perfect way to spend the summer.

While driving around the country, Claudia and I met a couple in their 50's that had bought a twenty-foot panel truck and were living on the road as contract drivers for Robert's Express (now part of Federal Express). Robert's Express at that time was a trucking company that specialized in rush shipments that were too small to warrant the cost of using a large truck and too big to put in a package. Because they were contractors they would carry loads only when they needed the money or when the destination was a place they wanted to check out. If they liked the destination they would stay put for a while before taking another load. If they were indifferent to the location, they would call the home office for an immediate load and head on to their next destination. In this way they were getting to see the country while being paid for it. Others have found similar opportunities delivering RVs, school busses and other large drivable objects that cannot be put on a truck. One young couple we know financed several years of overseas travel by teaching English to businessmen in Japan and by trading jewelry they purchased in India.

Our Strategy

In Claudia's and my case, my kids were out of college and on their own. We had sold our house and were comfortable with the amount of money we had set aside for our post-65 years. What relatively little income we needed while traveling was mainly covered by an investment strategy that we had in place. In mentioning investment strategies, it is important to note that investment opportunities, whether in real estate, a small business, or other, tend to be local in nature. What may work in the Midwest may

Taking "Substantially Equal Payments" from Your IRA Without Penalty

As you know, IRAs were established to allow an individual to build their retirement assets. Because the money is for retirement, there is a 10% penalty (in addition to paying any deferred tax) for taking a premature distribution before the age of 59½. There are exceptions to the 10% penalty rule for medical expenses, purchasing a first home, educational expenses, and for taking Substantially Equal Periodic Payments (SEPP).

Complete information on IRAs, including the exceptions to the 10% penalty rule is available from the Internal Revenue Service (IRS) in the following publication:

Internal Revenue Service — Publication 590
Individual Retirement Arrangements (IRAs)

The discussion on "Early Distributions" begins on page 49 of the 2003 edition of Publication 590. The basic rules regarding Substantially Equal Periodic Payments are that you can withdraw funds without being liable for the 10% penalty under the following conditions:

- The amount of annual withdrawal is based upon your age, the value of your IRAs, and an IRS Life Expectancy Table. The Life Expectancy Table can be found in Publication 590 and is used to ensure that you do not outlive your assets.
- Once you start periodic distributions you need to continue taking them for five years or until you reach 59½, whichever comes later.

One final note about taking funds from your IRAs — you only want to do this if you are comfortable with how much you have already set aside for a "traditional" retirement.

have no relevance in California. You will need to keep your eyes open for possible opportunities in your community.

When our investment strategy began to lose steam, we were able to rely on our savings and started taking early distributions from our IRA retirement accounts. *Yes, you can take early distributions from your IRA retirement accounts without penalty before the age of 59½ by taking "substantially equal payments."* We were comfortable doing this because we had an adequate amount set aside in our retirement accounts, and we have made sure that the amount we took out would not jeopardize the nest egg. Our combination of strategies was more than sufficient to cover our expenses while we were literally on the road. Now that we have settled down and have a house, the distributions and other activities have been able to cover enough of our still simplified expenses to make it not necessary to go back to a permanent fulltime job. We do have a gap and have been able to cover it through various consulting and contract work assignments. I now look at work assignments as an opportunity to fund another round of activities.

Your Strategy

When you do simplify your life to a manageable gap, you will find that if you have a financial reversal it will not have the same adverse impact that it would have had before you simplified. With a reduced run rate you will not be running up a large deficit if the cash spigot slows down. Conversely, when the cash flow improves, it will not take forever to recover. You will not have a huge hole that will be impossible to dig out of.

For your personal financial planning, you will want to take a serious inventory of your capabilities and resourcefulness in being able to cover "the gap."

- Are you willing to simplify your life?

- What are you willing to give up?

- What have you set aside in financial resources to generate income?

- What skills, talents, knowledge and interests do you have that you can use to generate income?

- How comfortable are you with uncertainty?

- How long of a dry spell can you endure?

- Are you willing to hustle to achieve your goals?

- How realistic is your assessment?

Your answers to the above questions will go a long way in determining if a more independent existence is practical or possible for you.

Even if you are not seriously thinking about seeking independence right now, there are many good reasons to understand the concept of "the gap" and the possibility of engaging in a portfolio of income-producing activities if only to protect yourself from the possibility of losing your job. Our economy has been shifting for many years and is still shifting, and the possibility of your job disappearing should always be in your planning.

For instance, I had a business acquaintance of mine in his mid-fifties who was working for a large corporation in the middle of a downsizing campaign. He was given a one-time-only buyout offer that would put a substantial amount of cash in his pocket. It was not enough to carry him for the rest of his life, but it was large enough to give him a head start. He was living in a medium-size metropolitan area and put out feelers locally for a similar job. Because he did not get any immediate job offers and because he still had one child at home, he declined the buyout.

When the buyout period expired, he soon realized that he had made a major mistake. He was now working in a lonely place. All of his contemporaries and all who knew his work and appreciated his contributions were gone. He was now working for someone not even in the same town and several years younger than he. His first assignment under the new regime was to dismantle every initiative he had worked on for the past ten years and to outsource those activities. The end result was to put the remaining people who had ever worked with him out of a job. With that messy piece of business completed, he was then given a "take it or leave it" transfer to a larger and more expensive metropolitan area. Since I lost contact with my acquaintance, his company has gone through two separate merger and acquisition events. Who knows how he fared in the turmoil?

So please remember, if your company offers you a buyout, your company has already determined that they do not really need you or particularly want you around. Do you really want to give the most important commodity that you have, your time, to people like that? Also, if you are offered a gift of cash, please consider taking it as an opportunity to jump start a new life because there are many ways of "being" that do not involve regular corporate employment.

CHANGING YOUR MINDSET FROM EMPLOYEE TO SMALL BUSINESS PERSON

Another thing to remember if you wish to maintain your independence from regular employment after you leave the road is to start thinking of yourself as a small business person. This means that there will be no more paid sick days, holidays or vacations, nor will you get paid while goofing off on the job. You will only be making money on what you actually do or establish. Your success at this will determine if you will be able to maintain your independence.

I know a musician who figured out at a very young age how to be independent and has made a very good life for himself for the past thirty years. His current routine usually finds him on tour performing in the spring and fall, hiking in the summer, and spending the winters near a ski resort. He told me that he knows many musicians who are much better than he but no longer perform. Some, he said, burned out, but most were not able to turn their profession or lifestyle into a business. In his case, his performances are unique which has created a niche following for him. He has learned how to promote his performances, sell his CDs, encourage people to use his web site, and use his music to support environmental causes that concern him. His ability to make a business of his activities has enabled him to achieve his independence and many other goals.

REMEMBER THAT THIS IS YOU WE'RE TALKING ABOUT!

You also have to be realistic. You have to start off with the recognition that this is your life that we are talking about, and whether you like it or not, you are still going to be you regardless of whether you stay at work or hit the road. There is no magical positive energy exercise or daily affirmation that is going to erase and remold a lifetime of experience. You are not going to go through a presto-chango process to acquire talent you do not have. Expecting to support yourself in the arts after spending the first 50 years of your life without exhibiting any particular artistic bent is probably not going to happen.

This should not discourage you from taking up a creative pursuit for your own enjoyment, just don't count on it to be your main source of funding. Paul Gauguin already had artistic talent before he abandoned his job as a stockbroker and took off for Tahiti to paint. On the other side of the coin, while in his 50's Ray Kroc was able to parlay his previous experience of selling in the foodservice industry to turn McDonald's into a household name and making himself fabulously wealthy in the process. The bottom line is that whatever enterprises you establish to maintain your independence will most likely be a continuation of what you are capable of doing right now.

My personal preference would be spend most of my time hiking in the backcountry studying archaeological sites, going on adventures, composing my thoughts, and chasing other interests. As much as I love doing them, they do not contribute to covering the gap. Until they do (and they probably won't), I will have to retain business activities that use my previous business knowledge in my portfolio of income producing activities. I recognize that my primary motivation for doing them is to cover the gap and to fund what I would rather prefer doing. But I guarantee you that if my hobby activities ever do cover the gap, my briefcase and business materials are going straight into the trash barrel.

*"Maybe I just didn't explain the nest egg well enough.
If you understood, it's a very sacred thing, the nest egg...."*

from the movie Lost in America

ASSEMBLING A "NEST EGG"

Unless you do not need money, you will need a nest egg to provide income for retirement, seed capital for a business or investment, and cash for current expenses. Your nest egg is the total of those resources that you can convert to cash or its equivalent. It includes investments and retirement accounts, and perhaps your house and other items you plan to sell as part of your simplification process or other items that you will no longer need if you are headed for the road. If you are not happy with the size of your nest egg, you can start the simplification process long before you actually hit the road and then add what you are no longer spending to the nest egg.

Once you assemble the nest egg it is important that you protect it and not jeopardize it. In order to understand the importance of the nest egg, your homework assignment for tonight is to rent and watch the 1985 Albert Brooks movie comedy—*Lost in America* (see opening quote above). I do not want you to come back to me to say that I did not adequately explain the nest egg theory to you.

Access to Capital

If you are not in position to immediately pay for an outstanding opportunity that may come your way from funds in your nest egg, you can extend the reach of your nest egg by having a good credit rating. This will provide you easy access to capital. By having access to capital you will have the flexibility to act upon an outstanding opportunity when or if one appears.

One of the great advantages of living in our country today is that unsecured credit in the form of credit cards and credit lines is readily available to almost everyone. An alternative to unsecured credit would be to have a Home Equity Line of Credit. Either one will get the job done. I am not advocating that you subsidize your lifestyle through credit and build up insurmountable debt at near usurious interest rates. I am suggesting that if you are prudent, you may want to have some credit available to be able to take advantage of an opportunity where you have a high degree of confidence in its success, and that it is one you can get out of quickly.

I want to reiterate and make it absolutely clear that I am not encouraging you to build up your credit card debt. I am only suggesting that you have available credit to provide you flexibility. If you do have credit card debt right now, reducing that debt should be one of your top priorities. As one person I know said it so well — "*it's not my expenses, it's my debts that keep me at work.*"

Before using your credit card or credit line to access capital, call the credit card company to find out what they charge for a cash advance fee and if there is a cap on it. That is, they may charge you three to five percent for accessing your credit line; however, if they offer a cap on the advance fee, the maximum charge may then only be $50 to $100. If there is no cap on the advance fee, ask them if they can offer you checks to write against your credit line and if there is a cap on the fee for using a check. If they still do not offer a cap, then cut up that card with a pair of scissors and throw it away. There are too many credit providers out there for you to accept or consider a credit line without a cap on the advance fee. Just keep looking until you find one that is right for you.

The impact of a cap on the advance fee is illustrated as follows:

Amount of Advance	$5000
Advance Fee %	4%
Maximum Advance Fee (Cap)	No Cap/Unlimited
Total Advance Fee	$200
Amount of Advance	$5000
Advance Fee %	5%
Maximum Advance Fee (Cap)	$50
Total Advance Fee	$50

As you see there is a big difference, and consider the size of the difference if you are taking a larger advance. It pays to shop around.

Case Study of Assembling a Nest Egg and Using Access to Capital

Earlier I mentioned that we had an investment strategy in place to cover a substantial portion of our gap. Our strategy was participating in the conversion of mutual savings and loans associations to stock companies. This opportunity has essentially come and gone, and when it did exist, it existed only in a few parts of the country. But for a brief moment it was quite lucrative. Participating in the opportunity required that you had deposits in as many mutual saving institutions that you could open, and that you had access to capital when, or if, stock became available for purchase.

When I first heard about savings and loan conversions, I did not have any spare funds. In addition to having most of my money tied up in bills, I had bought a new home and had children starting college. Somehow I found the money to open saving accounts. I deferred purchases, wore clothes longer, sold collections, emptied the penny jar, put travel expense reimbursement checks into savings accounts, sold frequent flyer coupons and did whatever I could to raise cash to open accounts. Over time I opened over one hundred saving accounts. There are two important lessons here for your planning. One is that when you are trying to build a nest egg, you look everywhere to see how you can raise funds and what you can covert to cash. The other is that you do not have to do everything immediately; do things over time as you can. The important thing is that if you have a strategy, you do it and don't just talk about it.

The second aspect of participating in savings and loan conversions was having funds to buy stock when (and if) it became available to account holders. In my case, my free cash was in savings accounts or tied up. I turned to credit cards to provide the funds that I did not have. I was willing to use credit cards because the majority of the profit on the stock would be made on the first day of issue. This meant that I could use credit cards to raise funds with the expectation that I could buy the stock, sell it, and pay back the credit cards within a few weeks. When I was actively participating in the stock conversions, I would respond to all the decent credit card offers that came in the mail to make sure I had adequate access to capital.

I was a small player in this opportunity, but I am happy with how it paid off for me. The lesson for you is that if you are not in a desperate situation and are willing to make personal sacrifices you can raise a nest egg. Those sacrifices could be doing without or taking on a second job. In a sense, the savings and loan conversions were a form of a second job for me. The next lesson is that if you are confident of an opportunity, again unless you are desperate, you can raise money to act upon it. As a precaution, you need to understand the risks and the amount of risk you personally can tolerate before engaging in any enterprise. What may be right for me or someone else may not be right for you. The final lesson is that you do not have to hit a home run for an opportunity to be of value. A series of singles can be just as effective in getting the job done.

Preparation—
Establishing an Infrastructure

Dance of the Double Woman, *c. 1950*
Oscar Howe, Yankton Sioux, 1915–1983;
Watercolor on paper;
Philbrook Museum of Art, Museum purchase
1950.11

"At any rate the Lord plays and diverts himself in the garden of His creation, and if we could let go of our own obsession with what we think is the meaning of it all, we might be able to hear His call and follow Him in His mysterious, cosmic dance."

New Seeds of Contemplation — Thomas Merton

A fter you have determined that you should and can adopt a more independent life and *play in the garden of His creation,* your next step will be to establish an infrastructure of serv- ices and devices to allow you to do so. Some of you may plan to spend a portion of your time literally on the road pursuing a series of lifelong dreams, some of you may plan to relocate to totally new surroundings, and others of you may just stay put. Regardless of your situation you will need to have an adequate infrastructure for keeping in touch in order to stay on top of your responsibilities, and to have the tools necessary for income producing activities to cover the gap. Your infrastructure will have much to say on your ability to be and to remain independent. Your ability to let go of much of what you may have considered essential will also have much to say on your ability to be and to remain independent.

In our case, our initial plans had us living literally on the road without a home. To support that we assembled an infrastructure that gave us a "virtual home" which we called our "virtual exis- tence." Our infrastructure allowed us to mange our responsibilities and to be mobile at the same time. We could be across the street or on the other side of the world without sacrificing effectiveness.

With a few modifications our basic infrastructure and use of resources later on enabled us to buy a home in an area that did not have the type of jobs that we were most familiar with. This is a very important point for your planning, because the reality of today's economy is that more and more "corporate" jobs are migrating to the larger metropolitan areas. This means that whether you will be driving on the road, floating on a houseboat, combing a beach, watching birds from a mountain cabin, or clearing a field on a farm, you can tap into that "metropolitan economy" with a good infrastructure.

Twenty years ago it would have been very difficult to tap into a "metropolitan economy" without being in the metropolitan center. Your living choices were pretty much limited to where you could find a job. The desirable/exotic locations were limited to those who grew up in the area, those who could afford to take a low paying job there, artists and craftsmen who could work out of their homes, the idle rich, or beachcombing drop outs. With today's technology it is now possible for many of us to have our chosen work in our preferred location.

YOUR INFRASTRUCTURE

Your infrastructure plans will begin with what to do with your house. Selling your house could be an important step in your simplification strategy or a source of capital to fund a nest egg. In our case, we had fairly specific plans that would keep us on the road for at least a year, and we were reasonably certain that when we settled down we would want to live someplace warmer and more mountainous than Chicago. We, therefore, decided to sell our house and to store our possessions. By doing so we had the additional benefit of reducing our living expenses to the point where we would not have to worry about supplementing our income-producing activities beyond our investment strategy while we were on the road. If your plans have you returning to your present location after spending time away, a better option for you may be to rent your house for the duration of your journey.

Once we made the decision to sell our house and store our possessions, we then went on to the next step of acquiring the services and devices to support our "virtual existence." With today's technology this is becoming easier and easier to do. It has now reached the point that other than for the socialization or for some face-to-face meetings, many of you may never need to step into an office again. In fact, I have had some friends tell me that there is very little socialization left in their office. This is because the administration staff was eliminated years ago and the balance of the staff is either based on-site at a customer or telecommuting from home.

OUR INFRASTRUCTURE

Items that we used in establishing an infrastructure are discussed below. Even if your plans call for you to stay in the same location, many of the items will still be applicable to establishing your independent existence.

Mailing Address

Because we would be without a home, we needed a place to use as a legal address and to receive mail. We also needed the ability to have our mail shipped to us when we needed it, wherever we were. Anyone who will be spending an extended period away from home will need to have some process for handling the mail and the accompanying bills. In our case we chose a mailbox at a nearby UPS Store (or MailBoxes Etc., as it was called then). Our legal residence became a four-inch by four-inch mailbox, and we changed all of our bank accounts, insurance policies, brokerage accounts, credit cards, library cards, driver's licenses, voter's registrations, et al. to that new address.

We could have chosen a mailbox at the U.S. Postal Service,

but for someone literally on the road a UPS Store, or other similar service, is a much better option. A UPS Store provides you a physical address. This is especially important for receiving packages. United Parcel Service and Federal Express will not deliver to a U.S. Postal Service box. Also, a UPS Store will sign for any packages, so you do not have to hang around to wait for an expected delivery. If someone were to ask you for your address, you will be able to give them what appears to be a physical street address rather than a box number. I just called my box number my apartment number.

Even more important to someone spending time away is that a UPS Store will ship your mail to you; the U.S. Postal Service will not. We called up our UPS Store from all over the USA and from Asia to get our mail shipped to us. If you do not have a specific address to give to the UPS Store for shipping your mail, you can have them send it to a nearby Post Office in care of General Delivery. In that case, all you need to do is to go to the Post Office and check to see if they have a package for you. By doing this we were able to keep on top of bills, personal business, and obligations regardless of where we were. You are now free to go anywhere in the world knowing that if you need to get your mail, you can get it without burdening friends or family.

To provide us more flexibility, we converted as many payments as we could to some form of automatic or electronic payment. This reduced the number of bills we received and had to pay by mail. To cut down on the amount of mail that needed to be boxed up and shipped to us, we contacted the major sources of our junk mail and asked them to stop sending it.

Along the lines of junk mail, one hidden benefit of not having a home was not being bombarded with mail solicitations and not having telemarketers call. I had quite a bit of fun in my last few months before hitting the road in telling telemarketers, *"I'm sorry, I'd love your offering, but I won't be able to use your service because I am disengaging from the material world to live in a tent."*

Unfortunately, when we did return to a house, it did not take long for the solicitors and callers to find us.

Cell Phone

The next piece of infrastructure is a cell phone. It is not mandatory, but it is very handy for those away to keep in touch. Not necessarily for receiving calls, but for the voice mail service it provides. In our case, we only turned the phone on when we had to make a call, or when we checked for messages. The value of the cell phone is that someone can leave you a message regardless of where you are. If you will be making phone calls while traveling, you will want a cell service plan that does not charge for long distance calls or for roaming when out of your provider's service area. This will protect you from an unpleasant surprise of finding out that you just spent $10.00 for a two-minute phone call.

If you prefer not to use your cell phone to make calls, you can save a considerable amount of money on long distance phone calls by using pre-paid phone calling cards. If you are traveling overseas, you will probably want to use a pre-paid calling card or your personal credit card when making phone calls. If you are traveling domestically, especially in rural or mountainous areas, a pre-paid phone card is a good back-up in the event a cell signal is not available when you want to make a phone call.

Another handy item about a cell phone is that it can allow you to have an area code for a place other than your residence. When we relocated to New Mexico, I was able to get some project work with an out-of-state company. They wanted me to have a phone number local to their place of business. No problem, with a cell phone with no long distance or roaming charges, I can sit in my home office in New Mexico and can be easily reached with a local phone call by the people I do work with. Better yet, if I do not want to be reached, I can turn the phone off and check for messages later. I had one friend in a sales position who was able to take his family on a four-month driving trip without missing a day of work just by turning on and turning off his cell phone.

An Example of Effectively Using Infrastructure

In the case above, my friend's daughter had just turned four, and he figured that once she started school it would be several years before his family would have a chance to tour the country. So he decided to take his family around the country before she started school. Not wishing nor being in a position to quit his job, he decided to have it both ways—continue working and tour the country with his family. In his case, he temporarily shut down his house, put everything that he needed in his van, and kept his job. He did have a leg up on the job front in that he was already working out of his house; so he just put his home office on wheels.

For his infrastructure he arranged to have his mail sent to his father's house and got his and her cell phones. That way if he and his wife ever got separated at a national park, shopping mall or some other place they would be able to contact each other. As for his work, his primary job activities as a salesperson had him talking to prospective customers over the phone, scheduling appointments when required, preparing recommendations and price quotations, working with people in the corporate office over the phone, and being responsive to internal and external requests. Almost all of these functions can be accomplished with a combination of a telephone, personal computer, email address, internet connection, and an internet fax service. If you have those tools available to you, it really does not matter where you are using them as long as you are getting the job done. Because he did not necessarily have access to an internet connection during much of the day, he arranged to have email messages delivered to his cell phone. In that manner he was able to be responsive throughout the day.

While on tour he and his family would stay at motels, with relatives, and sometimes with friends. In many cases they would rent a cabin or beach house for a few days. As for his general work schedule, he started the day off by getting his phone calls out of the way. Once that was done, it was time to head out for the day's planned activities. He did carry his cell phone with the ringer off to be aware of email and incoming phone calls. Unless they were critical, he would respond to them later; obviously, he would make time for prescheduled calls. In the evening, after the day's tour activities were done, he responded to his emails, faxes and calls that he missed. He also used that time to prepare correspondence, proposals, price quotes and the like. His email and internet fax service then allowed him to distribute all of his correspondence. In short, he did all of the work that was expected of him; he just did it in a time frame and location that would allow him to spend much of the day on tour. As a final touch, because his tour of the nation was being driven by the sales appointments he made, he was able to get his company to underwrite much of the tour's cost through reimbursed travel expenses.

As my friend's experience illustrates, a good infrastructure properly used, does allow you to be available (and responsible) while being elsewhere.

Personal Computer, Internet Connection and Email Address

Continuing on with infrastructure, as my friend's example brings home, email is a very convenient way to keep in touch and to conduct business while on the road. If you do not need a laptop computer for business, you can still have access to the Internet for your email messages. If you are overseas, you will find Internet cafes almost anywhere. If you are traveling in this country, you can go to a local library even in the smallest of towns or to a Kinko's Copy Center to access the Internet. Regardless of where you access the Internet you can benefit from having a web-based email address such as Hotmail. Even if you have an email address provided by an Internet service provider, it still makes sense to have a Hotmail address (or equivalent) as backup. That way you can always get your email regardless of what computer you are using.

If you choose to travel with a laptop computer, you will want to make sure that your Internet service provider has an adequate supply of local access phone numbers or an "800" number service. This is not an issue with the major Internet service providers like MSN or AOL. You will find that most places where you stay will have a phone jack for connecting to the Internet. Even many RV campgrounds and low-priced motels now have connections.

At the time of this writing the nation is rapidly being equipped for Wi-Fi (Wireless Fidelity). Wi-Fi essentially allows you to access the Internet without a phone or cable connection. It requires that your PC be equipped with a wireless adapter card and be within range of a Wi-Fi base station. Areas that have been equipped for Wi-Fi include offices, hotels, coffee shops, fast food restaurants, airports and other places where people can hang out. Eventually the whole world could be equipped for Wi-Fi. Many people are now using Wi-Fi to access the Internet with their laptop computer while they are hanging out or while waiting to catch an airplane. Wi-Fi could be a boon for those who need to work from home but find too many distractions at home to be effective. They can now take their home office to a neutral location and get their work done.

Conducting Your Life or Business on the Road

With a mailing address, cell phone, email address and Internet access, you can now be anywhere and be able to keep in touch and conduct business as well as if you were in the office. In our case, we were able to manage our investments, finances and responsibilities in addition to conducting business transactions while we were driving around the country, traveling overseas and even while hiking the Appalachian Trail because of our infrastructure. With the basic infrastructure and some supplemental business services one could, depending on their line of work, live on the road and still work if they wish.

A "Mobile" Office Will Not Necessarily Support Everyone

When discussing a "mobile office" consisting of a personal computer, cell phone, Internet connection and the like, what we are really talking about is a toolkit. If your background is working in an office environment, it is possible that much of your office toolkit can be relocated offsite to support an independent lifestyle. There are other skill sets that require a different toolkit. Some of them cannot be relocated offsite. Certainly if you are a dentist and plan to continue as a dentist, there is a good chance that you will not be able to drive around the country with a dental chair in the back of your pick-up truck and wait at roadside rest stops to clean and drill teeth to pick up some spare cash. If you are a high energy physicist, it is unlikely that you will be unable to build a multi-billion dollar cyclotron in your backyard to conduct high energy physics experiments. There are, however, other toolkits that you can relocate to your home or workshop for establishing a cottage industry to support and enhance an independent existence.

One man I know left his position as an engineer at a large utility company while still in his fifties to work as a gunsmith (a life-long hobby of his) in his own home-based workshop. When he left his job, he sold his company stock to buy some income property to provide a source of cash to

Examples Are All Around You

Throughout this narrative I have cited many people that I have run across in my life as examples to illuminate a point. I could have used many more. Examples are everywhere, and you certainly have run across many in your life. These are the people that you can learn from. What did they do right? What did they do wrong? How many of them did something that you would like to do? How many of them ran out of time? How many of them were not ready? What can you incorporate from their experience into your life? As you go through this process you may start to realize that if they can do it, why not you? Why should it always be someone else and not you doing something special?

help cover his gap. As his skills developed, he has acquired a reputation for producing desirable and collectible hunting rifles and now has a backlog of orders. He has made it a priority to keep his workload at a comfortable level in order to have time for other activities and to take several trips a year. Through his tinkering he has also invented a couple of gun-related products that he has been able to sell by placing small ads in gun collector magazines. His only regret is that he did not leave his corporate job sooner. He is an excellent example of someone who developed a portfolio of activities that combined his interests, skills and determination with a toolkit that he could set up in his own workshop to cover his gap. This combination has allowed him to establish an independent existence.

Infrastructure as a Marketing Resource

In addition to enabling a mobile existence, today's technology makes it possible for a home-based cottage industry reach a broader market. It is possible to register an Internet domain name for $35 a year. (Check out www.register.com on the Internet.) In addition to your own web site, there is eBay as an outlet for product sales. Although these new marketing channels will not automatically bring people to your door, they do make it possible for a home-based enterprise to reach a broader market. They do not preclude one from needing a desirable service and some marketing savvy. But for someone with a product in demand (like the gunsmith mentioned above), they are another and affordable outlet.

Our Use of Our Infrastructure While Away

I mentioned earlier that a major part of our ability to cover "the gap" was to participate in savings and loan conversions. These conversions happened while we were overseas, while we hiked on the Appalachian Trail, and while we were driving around. Each conversion required us to perform a series of activities before the transaction would be complete. Any failure along the way would blow the whole deal for us. Our infrastructure made it possible for us to successfully execute a transaction regardless of where we were. In one case, while on the Appalachian Trail, I had to get to a mountain top in North Carolina to get in line of sight to a cell tower to complete one of the steps. It was our infrastructure that allowed us to be where we wanted to be and to keep on top of our business.

Supplemental Business Services to Support Your Independence

In addition to a well-planned infrastructure, there are many other supplemental business services that you can use to maintain a mobile or independent existence. I have made good use of all of the below to support my independence. Some of these may be of benefit to you:

- Overnight and express delivery services from the U.S. Postal Service, United Parcel Service, Federal Express and others. These services allow you to deliver documents and materials quickly regardless of where you are. Lack of proximity is no longer a disadvantage.

- Photocopying and Business Centers, such as Kinko's, UPS Stores, or large office supply centers, for making copies, preparing presentation documents, scanning documents into computer usable files, and sending or receiving faxes. These services allow you to prepare a professional-looking document without making a large capital investment.

- Internet-based faxing services, such as www.efax.com, for sending and receiving faxes on your personal computer. This service saves you the cost of a fax machine and a separate phone line for the fax machine. It is handy if your personal business requires you to receive or send a large number of faxed documents. This service also saves you the time of running out to the nearest fax machine to send or receive a fax and paying for each fax.

- Large office supply centers, such as Staples, Office Depot, or Office Max, for obtaining whatever supplies you need.

- Neutral places, such as Starbucks or cafes in large bookstores, to meet and conduct business.

All of these resources make it possible to earn income or to support activities outside of an office environment.

OTHER RESOURCES FOR BEING ON THE ROAD

In addition to a toolkit, there are many other resources that you can use to enhance your journey. Although some of the items described below may be presented in the context of literally being on the road, it is the thought process of recognizing and using them as resources that's of value to anyone seeking their independence. Much of your success at being independent will depend upon how well you are able to recognize the resources that are available to you.

The Internet

The Internet was mentioned previously as being part of one's infrastructure for keeping in touch and conducting business. It is also a valuable resource for enhancing all phases of your independent experience. We use the Internet all the time to obtain information and to plan activities. It has been valuable to us regardless of our state of mobility.

When we were driving around, I decided to train for a marathon. I was able to download a complete six-month training program for preparing for the marathon. When we decided to follow U.S. 41 to its southern terminus in Florida, we were able to incorporate watching a space shuttle launch at the Kennedy Space Center by checking out the launch schedule on the Internet. When we decided to go to a total eclipse of the sun that would be crossing Venezuela, we selected our viewing spot on a Caribbean beach and planned our entire trip with information we obtained on the Internet. We had heard from many people that Rolling Stones' concerts were worth checking out, so we looked at their tour schedule to see where we would cross paths and bought tickets through the Internet.

Unlikely Resources for Enhancing Your Activities

The Internet is a resource that smacks you in the face, but there are also many easy-to-ignore resources that can enhance your independent lifestyle. A primary goal for me in seeking independence was to be able to have the time to discover and participate in a series of experiences or adventures — large and small, near and far. Part of being able to accomplish this was recognizing an apparent resource no matter how mundane it may seem to be. In some ways it is cultivating the ability of letting something find you rather than you searching for it.

There are the standard travel guides that provide background information on a community you visit. However, when visiting a new location, don't overlook something as unlikely as a local phone book. A local phone book will oftentimes have a section on the history of community, and sometimes just by flipping through the yellow pages you might be able to identify what is important to the area and how it differs from other communities. A local newspaper is another source of information. But certainly nothing can be as mundane as a tourist information brochure rack that you find in motel and restaurant entryways. I had previously ignored the racks because I had assumed that they were for family attractions that would not interest me. I then started looking at them and learned that for a very small investment of time I might be rewarded with a true gem.

We found a true gem when Claudia and I spent the night in Chamberlain, South Dakota (where Interstate 90 crosses the Missouri River) and noticed a brochure for a Sioux Indian Cultural Museum at a mission and Indian school less than a mile from our motel. Because of our interest in Native American culture, we checked out the museum the next morning. The museum was fine, but what really grabbed us were the paintings there by Oscar Howe, a Native American artist from South Dakota who died in 1983. We had never heard of him prior to our visit. While at that museum we learned that there was another museum devoted exclusively to Oscar Howe in Mitchell, South Dakota, a few miles up Interstate 90 in the direction we were going. We went to Mitchell and were further taken in by Howe's paintings.

Our stumbling on Oscar Howe was a combination of recognizing resources and of being independent. Had we not been independent while traveling across South Dakota we probably never would have learned about Oscar Howe. Had we been traveling while we still had regular jobs, we more than likely would have been constrained by the time frame of a normal vacation period and would have crossed South Dakota as fast as possible to reach a bigger destination. Even if we had spent the night in Chamberlain while on a traditional vacation, we most likely would have been in the car long before the mission museum opened in order to make our miles. Being independent has allowed us not to worry about rushing and to take the time to follow up on items of a whimsical nature. Sometimes they have turned out to be gems. On the other side of the coin, would we have been turned into pumpkins had we never learned of Oscar Howe? No, but I believe that our lives have been enhanced by knowing that his talent is out there. For me, this is what being on the road both literally and metaphorically has been all about—having the luxury of time to enhance our lives in many big and little ways.

Local Libraries

Libraries are another obvious resource for any community. In addition to providing a place to check for email messages, local libraries are great places to hang out during bad weather and a tremendous information resource for someone on the road. When we were driving around the country, the local library was one of the first places we would check out when we arrived to a town. As out-of-towners we could not check out books, but we were more than welcome to read books or magazines, to work on study or research projects, and to buy books from their used book sales rack. But one of the main reasons to check out the local library is the bulletin board. There you can learn about lectures, classes, movie screenings, special events, and other cultural happenings in the community. It is an opportunity to learn of things to remain connected to the world, and to see if there is something of interest that you have always wanted to see or experience or maybe never even thought of before.

In our case, during our travels we spent a lot of time hanging out in Flagstaff, Arizona and really liked the library there. On one stop in Flagstaff, we went to the library and noticed on the bulletin board that a group of Tibetan Buddhist monks would be blessing a new wing at the Museum of Northern Arizona in Flagstaff that same afternoon. They were traveling across the country to raise funds for their monastery in India. We had always been intrigued by Tibetan throat singing and jumped at the opportunity to actually hear it live and in person. Words cannot describe throat singing; it has to be experienced. If you close your eyes while listening to it, it can send you off in a meditative trance. We were glad that we stumbled on the performance, and it added to our list of many pleasant surprises that we continue to find.

As a point of interest, the Museum of Northern Arizona in Flagstaff is a privately funded institution and is one of the best anthropology and geology museums anywhere. It is a place for quiet contemplation and learning rather than an entertainment center with lots of buttons to push.

CONCLUSION

The groundwork is there waiting to be used. In addition to the resources mentioned here there are many others that have been left out, but the focus of this book is about supporting an independent life rather than being a guide for someone living in their RV fulltime. What this discussion on infrastructure and resources should point out is that we are fortunate to live in times when it is so easy to establish an infrastructure to support an on-the-road experience and to maintain an ongoing independence. We are also fortunate to live in times where access to information and resources for learning is so prevalent. These capabilities not only facilitate your independence, they can also help you remain connected to the greater world. This ensures that you do not lose sight of what is happening outside of your personal experience — a way of remaining in touch even if you have severed bonds with a conventional lifestyle.

What We Learned
From Living on the Road

Angel Falls, Venezuela.
Photograph by the author.

*"Today is tomorrow... Is there anything
I can do for you, today?"*

from the movie **Groundhog Day**

oth being on the road and the movie **Groundhog Day** are about learning. (If you have not seen **Groundhog Day** it is well worth putting on your "to do" list.) In the previous chapters we have discussed making the decision, planning the finances, and establishing the infrastructure to become independent. The next step is actually doing it and seeing what you can learn. In our case we learned many lessons beyond the basic ones that could be helpful for your planning and thinking process. As mentioned previously, our experience has had two components. The first was literally being on the road for an extended period of "away from home" activities. The second has been one of being in a more conventional location but still in an independent mode. Our lessons should have some application regardless of what you anticipate your independent experience to be. To help in sharing those lessons, I will discuss briefly the chronology of what we did while on extended travel to provide a context for presenting what we learned. As I said in the beginning, this book is not meant to be a biography or a re-hash of our daily journal. It's designed to be helpful to your thought process and not an irrelevant bore.

As noted in the planning area of the write-up, we started off with two major projects planned—a long trip to Asia and a long hike on the Appalachian Trail that we expected to carry us through the first year. Our last day of work in Chicago was October 15, 1996 and two days later we were on the road. We were headed to California and left for China on Election Day. We traveled independently in China for a month, and then made it to the Philippines to do volunteer work at an economic development center at the beginning of December. There, we got the opportunity to become actual parts of the local community rather than just being tourists passing through. When we finished our assignments in mid-January, we did some traveling in the Philippines. Then it was back to California at the end of January to pick up the car and to head east to start hiking the Appalachian Trail at the end of March 1997. We were having the time of our lives on the trail until Claudia broke her leg five weeks into the hike after 350 miles of walking. After scrambling and some quick rearranging, we traveled around the country, crisscrossing through Chicago for Claudia's doctor appointments, for the balance of the spring, summer, fall and winter. We then went to Venezuela to see a total eclipse of the sun in February 1998. After the eclipse, we did a bit more traveling before picking up the Appalachian Trail in early April from where we left off the previous year. It turned out that Claudia's leg was still weak and she had to stop hiking. I kept hiking, while Claudia followed me in the car for her own Appalachian Trail experience. We finished the Appalachian Trail at the beginning of September. After the hike, we moved our act to New Mexico where we settled down in November 1998. There we have taken on a different array of activities.

That's it—our two years of being literally on the road, but before going on with various lessons, let's spend a few moments talking about Claudia's broken leg. You have to remember that the Appalachian Trail was a major keystone in our plans for the road. We had quit our jobs and sold our home. We had cut the cord and were out there with no place to call our own. Now we had a major disruption to our plans; one could call it a catastrophe. To add

insult to injury, we had come a long way from where we had started on the trail. We had gone through aches and pains, blisters,
snow, endless rain and terrible cold. We were finally in hiking
shape and the weather was getting better. We were able to go
double the miles from when we started. I could now hike to the
top of the mountain without pausing. More importantly we were
finding everything we sought and more on our long distance hike.
We were in nature everyday; we were part of a hiking community,
yet were able to spend most days by ourselves with only the sun,
the air and the sounds around us; we were removed from the noise
and clutter of life; we were living a truly simplified life with complete clarity and were able to have a contemplative experience by
being engaged only in the present moment. I have never had a
more fulfilling experience.

Then bang, disaster, in one brief moment it came to an end.
We had been on the trail five days since we last had a shower and
resupplied. It had been almost two weeks since we took a full day
off to rest. It was a little after noon and we only had five more miles
to go before we would reach the road crossing where we planned
to hitch a ride into town for a well deserved rest day. Ironically, it
was the best weather day we had had on the entire hike. You could
go on to say that it was one of the few nice weather days of the hike
so far. Maybe too nice, and maybe Claudia was looking too forward
to a warm shower and good food. Maybe she was shuffling her feet
too much when her boot got caught under a root covered with
fallen leaves and her momentum and weight of her pack catapult-
ed her forward to snap both bones in her lower left leg.

Our hike had come to a screaming halt. Claudia had come
to a screaming halt. I was, perhaps, forty or fifty feet ahead of
Claudia when she yelled — "*I broke my leg.*" I didn't want to believe
it. I ran back to her and asked if she was sure. "*Yes, I heard it.*" I
then asked if she could still walk. "*No, it's broken.*" (I must have
been a complete idiot or in total denial when I asked that question.) Now what? We were up on a mountain, on a hiking trail five

miles from the nearest road crossing. The first thing we did was to take off our packs and make a splint to secure her leg. Next I used the cell phone to call for help. Because our area code had recently changed the local cell carrier would not put a call through. This was really not the best time or place to deal with procedure and bureaucracy so I gave up on calling. I then put the packs on the side of the trail and attached a note explaining what had happened. I lifted Claudia up, had her lean against me, and we slowly started working our way down the trail.

We had only gone a few steps, when another hiking couple, a few years older than us, came by. We told them the situation, and they said they would rush ahead as fast they could to get help. Before they left, we gave them our cell and beeper number just in case someone could get a call through. We then started struggling down the trail. After a few more steps, another hiker (Jack) came rushing down the trail. He had read the note and came to help. He was younger and stronger than me. The first thing we did was to study the map. There was an old logging/jeep trail about a mile and a half up the trail. It was generally downhill to the crossing and a potential connecting point for a rescue vehicle. I agreed to run to the crossing to see if the jeep road was still there and if it was usable. I covered the three-mile roundtrip quickly, and by the time I got back, Jack had made a stretcher out of our rain gear and some small branches. Unfortunately the wood was rotten and the stretcher did not hold.

Now it was on to plan B. Jack decided to carry Claudia over his shoulder in a fireman's carry. I would shuttle back and forth to carry our three backpacks. Because Claudia could only endure so much bouncing, we stopped every hundred yards or so. That enabled me to keep up as I went back and forth bringing the packs. A few minutes later another hiker, around my age and without a pack, came along. He agreed to carry one of the packs to the road crossing at the bottom of the mountain. We finally made it to the jeep crossing after three o'clock.

Just in case the first couple was not able to get help, I decided to run down the jeep trail to the bottom of the mountain to try and get help. Jack agreed to stay with Claudia, and I left the cell phone and beeper with them. Fifteen minutes after I started running down the mountain, the beeper went off. Claudia called the number on the beeper with the cell phone (this time the cell call went through). It was the Sheriff's Department saying that Search and Rescue was coming up the jeep trail in a Suburban to bring her down. They were coming up on the other side of the mountain than I was running down. Meanwhile other hikers were coming along to offer Claudia whatever assistance they could. It was only when I reached the bottom of the mountain that I found out that help was on the way, and a National Forest ranger gave me a ride to the local hospital to wait for Claudia.

While running down the mountain I kept thinking about how fast things can change. I had a very hard time believing what had happened. It was so quick. In one brief instant our hike and plans had shifted from everything going right to everything coming to an abrupt halt. It was a cold slap in the face, highlighting that nothing is guaranteed and that no matter how well you plan or prepare everything is fragile. It can just happen, and in that case there is nothing else to but to suck it up and just deal with it.

Search and Rescue got Claudia to the hospital sometime after seven. Claudia told me that they went very slow to make sure that her leg did not get jostled. She also told me how her blood pressure dropped dramatically once the rescue team got her into the Suburban. At the hospital x-rays confirmed that she had broken both bones in her lower leg and the attending physician decided that she should go to a larger hospital in a town twenty miles away. We rode in an ambulance to the new hospital. There Claudia was fitted with a toe to hip cast sometime after eleven o'clock at night, close to eleven hours after she broke her leg. We did learn one very important lesson, and that is no matter how alienating much of society can be, there are giving and helping people and communities in many corners of the world that are there for you when you need help. For this we will always be grateful.

With Claudia in a cast and the hike over, the next step was to figure out what to do. What do you do when you have no place of your own to go back to or a job to go to on Monday? As much as I wanted to be bummed out about the hike coming to an end, I knew I had to get over it. The first thing we did when Claudia got out of the hospital the next day was to rent a car and get a motel room to regroup. The first item of business was to close down the hike. The next was to figure out what to do. We knew that we had to drive to Claudia's parents to get our car. We also knew that we had to set up ongoing treatment for Claudia's leg with her doctor in Chicago. In Chicago we could retool our journey by swapping items in our storage locker and getting whatever else we needed.

As for what to do, we had our planning and infrastructure to fall back upon. We had our finances in decent shape. We had our list of activities and personal interests to start picking and choosing. The reality was that until Claudia got a smaller cast, which would be in a few weeks, she was not going to be very mobile. The good thing for us is that Claudia loves to read and as long as she had a tall stack of books near her side there would be plenty for her to do. There were projects on my list that were not particularly compelling to Claudia. She had no interest in long-distance bicycle touring. This would be the perfect time for me to start scouting out a bike route from Chicago to Washington, DC. Ever since I visited Washington and hiked a portion of the C & O Canal while in high school, I had wanted to figure out a way to ride a bike from Chicago to Washington using off-road trails as much as possible. While Claudia was reading and doing indoor things, I rode my bike checking out potential routes, and that was how we started the next chapter of our on the road journey. We started in Chicago and slowly worked our way east. I actually rode the route in its entirety after we settled in New Mexico.

Another activity that I worked on, while Claudia was stationary because of her leg, was to train for the upcoming Chicago marathon in October, five months away. A marathon is something I had always talked about doing ever since reading about the Boston Marathon in **Life** magazine when I was in high school. Now was the perfect time for me to do it—I was in good shape from hiking; I had the time to run the one, two or three plus hours a day depending upon where I was in the training program; and I had the bike for cross-training.

Since Claudia's doctor was in Chicago, we knew we would be crossing Chicago several times for cast changes and other treatments for Claudia's leg. We were able to round out our activities with a series of loop trips that would start and end there to return for Claudia's next appointment. In addition to our planned activities we had many business errands, places we wanted to check out, people to see, and other tasks that we wanted to accomplish. We never found our life without meaning or wondering what we would do today. We crisscrossed the country and were truly successful in making a life for ourselves on the road. We look back at those trips as an opportunity to do things that most people only dream about doing.

From the experience of handling Claudia's broken leg we learned that our planning and infrastructure worked, and that no matter what disaster came our way we would be able to make a life for ourselves. Even though our original plans did not go exactly as we expected, we accomplished a lot and had a great time in the process. Once again, our infrastructure allowed us to be anywhere in the world and still be as close as across the street. Our multi-tiered planning process allowed us to continue our journeys and rearrange plans depending on our circumstances. Our use of resources allowed us to make a life for ourselves no matter where we were. And perhaps most of all, we learned that if you like where you are you really do not miss any of your possessions. For us, fulfillment came from being connected to the moment rather than from things we owned.

Possessions

To carry on the discussion of possessions, we would oftentimes be asked if we missed our home or our possessions. Surprisingly, the simple and honest answer is, and was, no. The only items that we ever did miss in our two years on the road were a few books and some CDs. We were very surprised to the extent that our possessions were a non-factor in our life; they just never crossed our minds. They were not important to what we were doing. Part of the simplification process is discovering how much you can do without. You soon realize that you do not own things; they own you. This is especially true if you are carrying them on your back while on a long-distance hike. On the other hand, when we did move into a house and unpack our boxes, it was like rediscovering everything for the very first time and opening a bunch of Christmas gifts.

The reason that our possessions were not important is because we were engaged in the moment, and they were not part of the moment. I noticed when hiking the Appalachian Trail that you could easily spot a hiker who would soon be leaving the trail because they would start talking about what they did not have — certain types of food, comforts, television

Storing Your Possessions

Even though our possessions were not important to us while we were traveling around, we did not want to throw them away and start from scratch when we settled down. If you think you might do the same, you will need to find a place to store your possessions. In our case we selected a temperature controlled indoor storage facility with a large freight elevator. When you actually place your belongings in the locker make sure that items you might need are close to the door. In that way you can access them easily, or at least with minimum disruption. We found ourselves swapping items at the end of most of our trips. The only glitch we had was when a fire next door setoff the sprinklers in our building. We lost a couple of boxes to water damage. Fortunately they were covered by insurance; so buy the insurance offered by the facility.

shows, companions and the like. If what you are doing is important to you and you are engaged in it, you innately grasp that those other things that you do not have with you are fine, but they are not essential for where you are right at this moment. You realize that you can get to those other items when you get to them, but not right now. What you learn is that if you like where you are and what you are doing, material possessions are of little or no consequence.

Luxury of Time

Outside of the non-importance of possessions, the most important lesson we learned was having the luxury of time to do something the way we wanted to do it. Rather than being on a vacation or a leave of absence with a limited window of opportunity to complete an activity, we had no constraints (we were free and easy) with a wide open window to take as much time or to make as many attempts as necessary to get a task done right. It was this luxury that allowed us to find Oscar Howe or to return to the Appalachian Trail to finish our hike. Although Claudia could not hike the Appalachian Trail in its entirety, she had the luxury to change how she would do it so it became a peak experience for both of us. It was this luxury that allowed us to deal with the unexpected and to make lemonade from lemons when Claudia broke her leg.

Storing Your Car

Getting back to simple lessons and in keeping with the chronology of being on the road, a very mundane but important item to consider is what to do with your car if you will not be driving it for an extended period of time. It was one of the first tasks we had to deal with when we went to Asia for three months and again when we went on the Appalachian Trail. If you have similar plans, you will need to do the same. In our case we left our car with relatives. If your car will not be driven while you are gone, you can reduce your expenses by suspending your automobile insurance coverage. You will, however, want to keep the comprehensive portion of your coverage in force in the event the proverbial tree falls on the car.

Travel Light

When you do go on extended travel, travel light. Take only what you absolutely need. As long as you are not on an expedition to remote backcountry, you can get most anything you need along the way—even in third world countries. We made the mistake when we went to Asia of packing large duffel bags to cover our needs from northern China where it would be cold to the Philippines where it would be hot. We exhausted ourselves by lugging around our stupid duffels. We really felt dumb when we found out that we could have easily bought anything we needed, such as a winter jacket, while in Asia. Rather than carry winter jackets, we could have bought them in China for a ridiculously low price and given them away when we left the cold weather. If you are really attached to an item that you are no longer using, you can always box it up and mail it to a friend for safekeeping. You just do not want to carry the extra weight.

Independent Travel

Even if you are not experienced in traveling to less developed countries, you do not need to take an escorted tour to visit one. It is quite possible to travel independently. Independent travel does not have to be strictly the realm of young vagabonds. In addition to possibly saving money, you are opening yourself up to a potential world of adventure. By traveling on your own you have the opportunity to interact with the local community rather than being confined to an air-conditioned bus being spoon fed information. We found that with a **Lonely Planet Guide** or its equivalent we could get along fine, most of the time, on our own.

We were willing to sacrifice a certain amount of comfort and were willing to take on some uncertainty to add to the overall quality of our journey.

Even though we sometimes looked and acted like the "two stooges on tour", we believe that we got more out of our travels by being on our own. We often went days being the only "Westerners" in sight. We were such a rare commodity that people would ask us to pose with them in family pictures. With no other Westerners around and no local language skills, we were on our own with the **Lonely Planet Guide** to fend for ourselves.

In one of those situations we were in Tai'an, China at the foot of Mount Taishan, the most sacred Taoist peak. We had walked up and down the 6000 plus steps to the top of Mount Taishan and were ready to eat. We had read in the **Lonely Planet Guide** about a restaurant in town that specialized in Beijing duck that had an English menu. We decided to check it out. After a couple of false starts we finally found the restaurant. Claudia, being a vegetarian, ordered some vegetables, and because I would not get any help from Claudia in eating a whole Beijing duck I ordered a smaller duck dish. My dish was quite good, but I couldn't help noticing how good the Beijing ducks being rolled out to various tables looked. I wondered if I had made a mistake in not ordering one. But because I was full from my meal, I allowed good judgment to overtake me, and we got up to pay for our dinner. Immediately, several waiters rushed over and rapidly waved their arms to motion us to sit down.

We had no idea why they would not let us leave, but we took their advice and sat down again. Moments later, a whole Beijing duck was rolling our way. I wondered if the people next to us had ordered the Beijing duck, and still wondered why they would not let us leave. The cart wasn't going to the table next to us. It was stopping at our table. It turns out that they weren't letting us leave because we were getting a whole duck as part of our meal even though we had already eaten. The waiter proceeded to carve the duck in front of us and arranged the head and neck in a decorative position. The waiter then brought out a large bowl of broth and duck parts to serve as our soup, and then placed heaping platters of duck meat in front of us. As suspected, and now confirmed, Claudia would not touch the duck. I was on my own, and not wanting to hurt anyone's feelings I ate the whole duck. Gagged to beyond the point of having a buzz, we were finally allowed to pay for our meal and released to venture out into the night.

The next day, when it was time for lunch, we decided to go back to the duck restaurant because the food was good and the menu was in English — so we would know what we were ordering. But this time we had it figured out. We would not order a duck dish because ordering a duck dish would mean that we would get another whole Beijing duck, and one major pig-out, or should I say duck-out, in a twenty-four hour period is enough. But in keeping with the spirit of a pig-out, I did order a pork dish. We ate our meal and got up to pay. Again, we were motioned to sit down, and again a cart with a whole Beijing duck was rolling our way. Claudia said that it looks like you're getting another duck. I replied that's impossible because I ordered pork, but I was wrong. The cart did stop at our table, and again we were presented with a whole duck with its head and neck arranged in a decorative manner. Again, Claudia would not help out, and again, I was forced to eat a whole duck. How I did this without using a crowbar to make room in my stomach and then having it pumped out afterwards, I do not know. But I did learn one thing — when you go into the duck restaurant in Tai'an, China, regardless of what you order they are not going to let you out of there until you eat a whole Beijing duck. Neither **The Lonely Planet** guide nor the English language menu had that little warning. So go there hungry, especially if you are traveling with a vegetarian.

Besides an adventure in every experience, independent travel does truly offer the opportunity to interact with the local populace. After the second duck-out at the duck restaurant, we, or at least I waddled to the railroad station to catch a train for a twenty-hour ride to Xian—the home of the Terracotta Army. We were traveling hard sleeper. In hard sleeper the rail car has a walkway against one wall while the other wall is sectioned off with thin dividers. Each section has two triple-decker bunks with a thin mattresses and bean bag pillows facing each other. We were the only Westerners on the train. When a young officer of the Peoples Liberation Army saw us when he entered the train, he had his seat switched to our section. He spoke some English and wanted to practice his language skills. The train was not very clean (filthy would be an appropriate descriptor) or particularly comfortable (some would say uncomfortable), and when we passed through snow in the mountains, we discovered the train was not heated as it became very cold. But the ride was unforgettable because as many people as possible, probably close to twenty, forced themselves into our tiny section. They wanted to learn about our life, and they asked the army officer to relay various questions to us. We answered and the officer would then announce our answer in Chinese to the small assembly. We passed most of the night exchanging stories, learning and sharing food. If our entire three months in Asia had nothing else to offer, that one train ride would have made quitting our jobs and traveling overseas worthwhile. This is what being on the road was and is for me.

Another advantage of independent travel is the opportunity to meet kindred spirits. You will meet them in places where vagabonds (long-term travelers) tend to hang out. When we were in China, the two big hangouts were Dali, not too far from Tibet, and Yangshuo, set amidst the limestone karst peaks of southwest China. (It was on a boat trip to Yangshuo in a prior trip to China that I met the couple mentioned earlier in this book who were going to southwest China to study tortoiseshell plastrons and who became my instant heroes and inspiration for independence.) Most of the independent vagabonds we met were European or Australian. Because of shorter vacations and more serious

Independent Travel

This book is in no way a replacement for a good travel guide and is not meant to be an instruction guide on how to travel. There are a few items worth covering that could be valuable in your overall planning efforts. Some of them are:

- Have a good grasp of the "basic essentials" while traveling—know your culinary trouble spots in order to avoid unwanted illness; bring along light hiking shoes and a daypack for walking around; if the water is bad, make sure that you only drink bottled water; and don't forget to bring along peanut butter and jelly just in case you cannot find food that you are willing to eat.
- Be aware that "over traveling" can cause travel burnout. To avoid this, focus only on a small number of stops. With a manageable number of stops, you can have time to hang out and explore (drill down) the local environs. If you try to go everywhere you will not only burnout but become punch drunk and start saying, "haven't we seen this already?"
- For your itinerary planning, consider using a package tour brochure to identify a country's highpoints. After selecting the highpoints you wish to check out you can then use your Lonely Planet Guide to fill in the gaps, to provide the details, and figure out how to get around.
- If your initial overseas arrival will be in the middle of the night it makes sense to have a hotel reservation. If the hotel you reserved costs more money than you care to spend, you can always switch the next day when you can see what is around you. If your arrival will be during the day, you can forsake the hotel reservation and use the airport hotel desk to find a hotel when you arrive. Most international airports have a hotel desk, and they can oftentimes get you a better rate than if you just show up at the hotel.
- If you have a medical or financial emergency while overseas, you can use a large hotel in a major city to regroup. There you will have a comfortable lobby to think about what to do. You will likely have access to someone who speaks your language, telephones for making an overseas phone call, banking services to get money, and a travel agent to book a flight.
- Finally, as you meet fellow trekkers in your overseas travel you can expect the following putdowns:

    "You've only been here for X days; we've been here for X+ days."

    "Your pack weighs X pounds; ours only weighs x."

    "You paid that much for that; we only paid X"

    "You should have checked out ___ when you were there."

    "You should have been here in the (your decade of choice)."

attitudes toward work, very few were Americans. Many of these vagabonds have built their entire life around their personal adventures. From these kindred spirits you can learn of places to go, experiences to seek and ways to stretch your funds to keep you on the road longer.

Living in a Local Community

Our main purpose for going to Asia was to help out at a local economic development center in the Philippines. Our dream was to have the opportunity to live in and to become part of a community that was completely different from our former home. It is one thing to travel and pass through an area. It is a totally different experience to actually stay put. After a certain amount of time, even though we were different, we hoped to become accepted as part of the landscape.

We did become part of the landscape—perhaps, more as a curiosity rather than as a friend. When it became apparent that we were not going to disappear, we became more accepted. It was at that point that we could begin to start understanding another culture. You may find much that you disagree with and wish you could bang someone's head to change it. But at the same time you start to see why various conditions exist because of their experience. Rather than judge, it is best to observe and absorb the rhythm of what is going on around you.

We learned that many people in the Philippines have an attitude towards ownership that is different than ours. As soon as someone starts to have more, friends, neighbors and family will start to "share out" the excess, and soon that person with more will no longer have more. Consequently, if you have a phone, you lock it up so someone doesn't share it to make an expensive overseas phone call. If you have a store with merchandise, you have an armed guard on-site to make sure someone does not share the merchandise. Because extra money will end up being shared, people would rather throw a big party (a "blow-out") than to save it for the future. As a consequence of the cultural underpinning of sharing and spending rather than saving to accumulate investment capital, a large amount of the commerce of the Philippines is controlled by ethnic Chinese or foreign investment.

In addition to learning about the underlying culture, you start to see how other people live their everyday life. We were invited to attend many local basketball games played outdoors on the lumpy hard packed dirt. Try dribbling a basketball on your backyard lawn. Being from Chicago, we were always being asked if we knew Michael Jordan. Although cock fighting is legal and a big sport in the Philippines, there are many local and illegal underground cock fighting pits and gambling dens. I was able to go to these. When a neighborhood child died, we were invited into the family's nipa hut to join in the consoling. On a happier note, Claudia was asked to be part of a wedding party as one of the attendants. These are only some the experiences that we never could have had as a tourist on an escorted tour with our noses pressed against the window inside of an air-conditioned bus.

So please, before you write out a check for a deposit on an escorted tour, pick up a **Lonely Planet Guide** to see if you might be able to do it yourself.

I have had many moments on both sides of the ocean that have reinforced my decision to choose independence. Within the context of independent travel there is one that stands out. It was on our fourth day in the Philippines. We were riding in a banca boat (a form of motorized outrigger canoe) to visit a small island to perform one of our tasks for the economic development center. It was early December, the sun was shining and the temperature was in the low 80's. The water was crystal clear and almost the same temperature as the air. While I was running my fingers through the water and staring at schools of brightly colored fish darting in and out of the coral, I kept thinking to myself about what I would be doing if I were still working. The trip to Asia would have been over long before I would have had the chance to ride on the banca boat, and I would have been back in Chicago. There the winter clouds would have already arrived to block the sun, and if the snow and cold had not yet come, it would not be long before they would. I then looked at the palm trees on the approaching island and I thought to myself— this is really nice and how grateful I am for the opportunity to change my life.

Making a Life for Yourself on the Road

At the conclusion of our Asian travels, we then spent much time on the road on this side of the ocean. The first thing to recognize in making a life for yourself on the road is that many people — full-time RVers, truckers, professional dirt bike racers, long distance hikers, drop-outs, performers and others — are living on the road on a near fulltime basis. Because there are so many people on the road there are more than adequate services — places to stay, places to keep clean, places to do your laundry, places to obtain food and ways to connect to the greater community — to support yourself on the road. Your job will be to blend those support services with your plans and interests to make a life for yourself on the road.

With our change in plans after Claudia broke her leg to have a series of loop trips, it would have made sense for us to travel in a small RV. We did not have an RV and made do with our car (a Ford Explorer). We had the option of camping out in a tent or staying in motels. Because of Claudia's leg, we tended to stay in motels. There is lodging to suit anyone's tastes, expectations, and finances. We found "extended stay" lodging to be very helpful when hanging out in a location for a longer period of time. "Extended stay" lodging provides you a work surface and cooking facilities. They are great for working on projects, saving on restaurant costs and making sure you eat properly. If you are camping or traveling in an RV, there are many campgrounds available to you. Many of the motels and campgrounds where you will be staying will have laundry facilities for keeping your clothes clean. Even if you are a hard-core dropout and never plan to see the inside of a motel, there are places to keep your clothes and yourself clean while on the road. Most large truck centers have laundry and shower facilities. Some of those truck centers even have Sunday morning church services.

Living on the road does not mean that you have to be constantly on the move from sun up to sun down. Living on the road is learning how to blend your responsibilities, projects, activities and interests while being away from a permanent job or residence. Time on the road could be traveling from place to place, or hanging out in one place, or a combination of the two. The most important aspect of making a life for yourself on the road is to have a variety of things going on so that you will always be engaged and never bored.

What helped us make a life for ourselves on the road was that we have many interests independent of each other. Making a life on your own is an important consideration for anyone contemplating an independent life. In our case, we are not velcroed at the hip like a pair of Klingons from Star Trek. We enjoy each other's company, but we can function quite fine when the other is not around. We do not need to make the other do what we are doing or to hold the other one back from doing what they want to do. This was especially helpful for us on the second time around on the Appalachian Trail. As I mentioned earlier, we picked-up the trail from where Claudia broke her leg the previous year and restarted the hike. After two weeks, Claudia's leg was too sore to continue hiking, and she got off the trail.

She did not need me around to catch a bus to go back to her parent's house to get the car, to visit with friends and family, to adopt a dog, and to run some business errands before catching up with me a couple of hundred miles up the trail. Claudia then followed me in the car as I hiked north. Her life was not one of boredom while waiting impatiently for me to walk the remaining

1400 plus miles of the trail. She had her own life. She was able to blend running, reading, prowling around in small towns and some hiking to make her own Appalachian Trail experience. In that way, it became a peak experience for both of us.

If you and your partner are not able to make lives independent of each other, while being together on the road or living under the same roof, one of you will likely end up being the entertainment director. Unless one of you has a lobotomy, the resulting resentment will soon put an end to your experiment, and possibly, to your partnership. It is important that each person has their own objectives, and both of you will need to work at not turning your adventure into one of you dragging the other one around.

Planning Your Travels and Activities

I cannot reiterate enough that we never ran out of things to do. In addition to our travels we were able to be where we needed to be to meet our responsibilities. For your planning you will want a map and a calendar. Even if you will not be undertaking extended travel, the same principals will apply to your experience. You will want to go through an iterative planning process that would start with major activities and work its way through family and personal obligations (anniversaries, graduations, holidays, . . .), business obligations (doctor's visits, tax preparation, business meetings), and personal commitments (marathons, plans with friends or family, . . .). As you identify various activities and events you will be building a framework of where you will be and when. Underlying that framework will be your basic daily activities (running, reading, study projects, managing finances, conducting business, and the like) that would take place no matter where you were. With a framework taking shape, you can then go back to your lists of interests and other objectives to overlay a series of activities and events that will accommodate the geography you will be covering. In that process, there will be specific dates associated with your various levels of activities. Those activities with specific dates will have the effect of driving a stake in the ground of where you want, or need, to be on a certain date. With stakes driven in the ground you can now let your travels and activities unfold as they happen.

Driving stakes into the ground was invaluable to our planning. It gave us some structure and allowed us to do some planning to maximize our use of time without sacrificing spontaneity or surprises. A case in point for us is that I planned to run in the Chicago Marathon in October, and we hoped to see a space shuttle launch five weeks later in Florida. That gave us a framework of time and geography to work with. We decided that that would be a perfect time for us to hang the southern portion of Highway U.S. 41 from our list of possible projects on to our framework. The five weeks duration also meant that we did not have to rush and could follow whatever whim caught our fancy. There are two words that can describe those five weeks — absolutely fantastic. We took our time. There was a stretch through Georgia while we followed the route of Sherman's army, where we were only averaging 40 miles a day — a little more than twice the speed of walking and a little less than half the speed of biking. There were many items from the database that we checked out, but of greater importance there were many many surprises that just blew us away. Among them was going to a wolf park in Indiana; meeting and talking to a World War II prisoner of war about his experience while visiting Andersonville (a Civil War POW camp in south Georgia); stumbling into a state park dedicated to the music of Stephan Foster where U.S. 41 crosses the Suwannee River (as in *Way down upon the Suwannee River...*); and spending the morning with hundreds of abandoned cats on a stretch of beach in Florida. Some of what surprised us may seem like a big "so what" to you, but I only mention them to illustrate that if you take your time, you may find many surprises to your liking. Part of your success in being independent will depend on your ability to find something new and exciting everyday to make your time and activities daily adventures.

While You Are Driving

Again, this is presented in the context of extended travel, but the principal of opening yourself up to what is around you is critical for sustaining your independence. If you are on the road in our country, there is a good chance that you will be driving. Some people may think of a long drive as being tedious and dread the thought of extended time in the car. I disagree. While on the road, just being curious and having interests can make even the most mundane an adventure. When driving on what appears to be a monotonous stretch of highway, have you thought about just observing and letting your eyes take in information? You may start to notice the ever-changing landscape. If you look closer you may notice that some areas are fertile while an adjacent plot of land may never have been touched by a plow. You could be blasé and uninterested, or you may be truly curious and think to yourself— just why is that so? You may notice something—a crop, a land-scape feature, an old right-of-way, an abandoned structure, or an unexplained bump in the ground and wonder — just what the heck is that? You may look at the land and wonder what it was like before it was settled? You may wonder what brought settlement to that location in the first place? Or, you may see a road, a ridgeline, or a path and ask yourself—just where does that go? The more questions you have, the more you will find of interest and the more you will find yourself engaged in the immediate moment. A journey will no longer be something to endure; it will become a mystery and an adventure to be savored. You may also be setting yourself up for whole series of new events to put on your schedule for just finding out the answers to your questions. You will find that there is never a shortage of things to do, just time to do them.

Letting Events Direct You — Going with the Flow

As previously discussed, you will want to have some structure in your planning and then let curiosity fill in the details. There will be times when there will be little structure, and you can let events unfold to see where they take you. An example for us was with one of our loop trips where we really did not have any stakes other than that we had to be back in Chicago at a certain time for another one of Claudia's doctor visits.

We started off by visiting one my sisters in Milwaukee and then headed west to check out some Indian effigy mounds and some Frank Lloyd Wright buildings. While crossing Wisconsin, we heard on the radio that the Lumberjack World Championships would be held in the north woods town of Hayward, Wisconsin later that week. Because Claudia had always wanted to see a lumberjack competition, we put that on our immediate to do list and set our sights on Hayward. While at the championships, we saw some very big men and women who you would not want to tangle with in the competition. They did not let us down with their ability to swing an axe or handle a chainsaw. We almost swallowed our hearts when one of the contestants in the tall pole climbing contest fell over 90 feet to the ground. Fortunately there were some pads, and the contestant did not die — at least not in front of us. He was still breathing when he was wheeled out on a stretcher to a waiting ambulance.

With the lumberjack events under our belts, we set our compass direction north and east. I had heard that the mining center of Sudbury, Ontario north of Lake Huron was the result of a large meteor impact many millions of years ago. With our already being in northern Wisconsin, this seemed like a good time to check that out. After Sudbury, we set our sights on upstate New York by way of Montreal. While sitting at a lunch counter in Fort Ticonderoga, New York, I picked up a newspaper and read in the Sports section that it was "Hall of Fame Weekend" in Cooperstown, New York, only a couple of hours away. Nellie Fox of the 1950's White Sox, who was (and still is) my all-time, all-time favorite baseball player, was going to be inducted. I had considered his delayed induction to the Hall of Fame a serious injustice, and had vowed many times that I would not step into Cooperstown until they admitted Nellie Fox. Here was my chance to turn my words into action. We were now on our way to Cooperstown.

With all of the visitors to Cooperstown, the closest room that we could find was over twenty miles away in a battered old motel with its price sufficiently marked up to over $70.00 a night for the occasion. We did, however, get a free breakfast of two dried out Hostess donuts with powdered sugar and got to meet two great pitchers, Don Newcomb and Joe Black, from the old Brooklyn Dodgers who were staying in the room right next to us. The Hall of Fame induction was an ultimate nerd experience and so much better than I expected.

From Cooperstown we set our bearing to the west and a bit south. We went through New York and Pennsylvania checking out many items and doing some business. We finally cleared Pennsylvania and were approaching Cleveland. There we decided to stop and check out the Rock and Roll Hall of Fame and Museum. The museum was fine; it would have been better in the fall when the kids would be back in school. The featured special exhibit was on the *Psychedelic 1960's*. Just as I was about to take a bite out of my sandwich in the lunchroom, Muhammad Ali, one of the biggest icons of the Psychedelic 60's, walked into the room. He was being given a special tour of the museum and the exhibit. I had seen Ali (then Cassius Clay) win the championship from Sonny Liston and had also seen most of his other big fights of the 60's on theater TV. In addition to boxing he was a major part of the era when I was younger, and I was compelled to go up and shake his hand, or I should say have my hands swallowed up by his. I absolutely felt puny next to him, and I am not that small. The effect of his Parkinson's disease is very dramatic in person; it's almost as if there is someone else inside trying to come out through his eyes in an otherwise vacant face on an unstable body.

After meeting Muhammad Ali we only had a couple of more stops before we completed our loop and ended back in Chicago for

Claudia's next doctor's appointment. For a period of time that was completely unplanned and not supposed to be particularly interesting, we had many surprises and many personally meaningful events. All of our trips had similar results. They were successful because we tried to keep our minds open to change and sometimes just let things happen. They were also successful because we mixed in specific goals to avoid drifting. We were rarely disappointed, and again we consider ourselves fortunate. The same flexibility and openness will help make your independence a success as it passes through its various phases.

In thinking about that loop trip I have often wondered if it was luck that the radio station that we were listening to in Wisconsin mentioned the Lumberjack Championships. Was it luck that we happened to be in upstate New York on Hall of Fame weekend and that Nellie Fox was being inducted into the Baseball Hall of Fame? Certainly if there had been any change anywhere along the way, we would not have run into Muhammad Ali in Cleveland. In fact, we were held up a day in Canada for car repairs. If that had not happened, how would the trip have turned out? And certainly if Claudia had not broken her leg we never would have been on that loop trip. Again, I have to ask myself if it was pure luck, or if Branch Ricky (the old-time baseball executive) was right when he said, *"Luck is the residue of planning."*

Managing Downtime

In talking about being on the road, I have mentioned a lot about travels. I need to point out that Claudia and I are not necessarily museum and tourist type people. We structure our activities around our interests and generally avoid blatantly tourist type destinations. We also recognize that there are some items, such as the Grand Canyon, the Great Wall of China, and a total eclipse of the sun, that are so impressive that they can only be truly appreciated when experienced in person. We also recognize that we do not want to suffer from travel burnout by spending time on things we could not care less about or could just as well experience by watching it on TV. Although we made every attempt to make sure that our time was full, we were not looking to kill time with what we would believe to be trivia. You will have to make the same type of decisions for managing your on the road experience.

A key element of success in your on the road experience, whether it is on extended travel or in your home, will be learning how to manage downtime. Sometimes downtime will be by choice or by happenstance. It may be a time between major projects. It may be while hanging out in one place to avoid travel burnout. Managing downtime will be finding meaningful activities for when you are not in motion. Again your lists of interests and general personal maintenance will come to the rescue. In our case we relied upon business projects, study projects and reading to best use our downtime. An example of downtime would be when we were in the Philippines. We went there with a series of assignments. When there were lulls between assignments or delays in completing an assignment, we had some downtime. I used that time to read several literary classics that I had always meant to read but never had.

As we have been exposed to different ideas, we have added learning more about them as future downtime activities. In this way our list of goals and objectives has continued to grow rather than shrink. I am not specifically advocating that you must read good books or engage in research. In fact I would caution that reading about something, or looking it up in the encyclopedia, does not automatically make you an expert on the subject. Many topics will require years of study before you might even come close to having a level of understanding or proficiency. What I am suggesting is that if you develop a wide and ever increasing range of interests, you will always have something to do whether you are in motion or not. What I am also suggesting is that you will want to find activities that will keep your level of intelligence up. Many people that you will meet on your journey through life may not be as reflective as you are; therefore, you may want to find other activities to keep your mind engaged to ensure that it is always sharp. Downtime is a good time for that, and it will be your ability in using your time while not in motion that will determine your suitability for a life on the road or independence. One of your responsibilities as an independent person will be controlling and filling your calendar and agenda.

Interaction with Other People

When you leave the world of fulltime work, you will be leaving a major part of your socialization network. If you have a need for socialization you will have to find other outlets than a fulltime job. If you spend extended time on the road, you will find some activities will lend themselves to meeting and interacting with other people while others will not. When traveling overseas as an independent traveler, you will have the opportunity to meet many interesting people. Meeting people is one the prime benefits of traveling overseas. Surprisingly, I also found a very close community on the Appalachian Trail. It was an opportunity to spend much of the day alone and still be part of a larger community. Other long-distance hiking experiences may be different.

While traveling around the country in our car, we did not meet many people. Driving a car and staying in a motel room can sometimes be an isolating experience. If you want to meet people and learn of others' experiences, you will need to go to places where you can hang out and not be separated by walls. Campgrounds and national parks are good places for this. We met many people living on the road at Big Bend National Park. Some of the people that you will meet in that kind of environment may be a bit close to the edge, but there are others that you will find more to your interest and liking.

If meeting new people is an important part of your experience, you will want to arrange your activities to ensure that you meet people. You may want to consider either overseas travel or a series of projects that will allow you to hang out for a certain amount of time at specific locations. Something along the line of the people I mentioned earlier who spent their fall in Yellowstone, their winter at the Everglades and their summer on the Appalachian Trail. There are also many participation and learning activities offered by Elderhostel, the Audubon Society, Habitat for Humanity and other groups that would allow you to both travel and interact with other people. A nice thing about interacting with other people is that you may pick up ideas for enterprises or learn of things to check out. It is a way to continue to grow.

If you are not traveling there are many ways to interact. This is especially valuable if you are relocating to a new area. There are educational opportunities, special interest organizations, advocacy groups and volunteer opportunities to consider. In my case when I moved to New Mexico I wanted to get involved in archaeology. To do so I took both continuing education and regular university archaeology classes, attended archaeology talks, and volunteered with the Bureau of Land Management to participate in archaeology site surveys being conducted on Bureau lands. I even took advantage of my Appalachian Trail experience by giving talks to hiking organizations and at outdoor stores. Through those involvements I have made friends with people who share these interests and who have increased my scope of knowledge. Your involvements could provide you the opportunity to do something similar.

Moving On to Another Phase of the Road

Unrecorded archaeological site in New Mexico.
Photograph by the author.

"I left the woods for as good a reason as I went there. Perhaps it seemed to me that I had several more lives to live, and could not spare any more time for that one.... I learned this, at least, by my experiment: that if one advances confidently in the direction of his dreams, and endeavors to live the way he has imagined, he will meet with a success unexpected in common hours."

Walden — Henry David Thoreau

There is a good chance that your independence experience will have many phases, or that you have several more lives to live. Those phases could be separated by the completion of a long-held goal, concluding a period of extended travel, starting a new enterprise, or something else. One of your responsibilities will be to recognize when it is time to wrap up one phase and shift on to the next. In our case, it was never our intention to remain literally on the road for the rest of our lives. We wanted to spend time away to accomplish several activities that we could never consider while engaged in a fulltime job. To a great extent we succeeded. One of our projects while on the road was checking out where to live when we completed our travels. I need to point out that we still have a long list of projects to complete, and still consider ourselves *on the road* — just in a different way.

There were several reasons for changing our way of being on the road. First and foremost, it was time to connect to a community in an area where we wanted to live. In our case it was the Southwest. The second reason was to develop other enterprises to replace the

What About You?

- Is there something you would like to study or learn more about?
- Are there skills you would like to develop?
- Is there something you would like to become involved in?

income that was no longer being provided by our investment strategy. In addition to replacing the income, we wanted to generate additional funding for new rounds of projects. We also wanted to engage in some new projects that we could not do while traveling around the country. Specifically for me I wanted to learn more about archaeology and to study a martial art. Those could not be done without staying put. For the archaeology, as mentioned, I have taken classes and have been active as a volunteer. I have also developed a hobby of taking my dogs into the backcountry looking for previously unrecorded archaeological sites. In my own little way I hope to make a contribution to the understanding of our pre-history along with having some fun in the process. In studying a martial art, I have learned that it is not something you learn after six easy lessons. It is something that you have to practice several days a week for several years to have any hopes for proficiency. I have also learned that I not particularly proficient at it and have further learned that one does not have to be particularly good at something to find value in it.

On the income generation side, I assessed my skills and determined that my best bet initially was to do some work that was related to my previous field (Information Technology) and area of expertise (Integrated Business Systems) on a consulting or contract basis. I was not interested in a permanent fulltime position. In contacting former co-workers I was able to learn of potential opportunities and found suitable work. If one of your phases on the road calls for you to earn some money, you will have to make a similar assessment. Not all backgrounds will have the same opportunities for contract or consulting work as mine did. If that is your situation, you will then need to determine how your skills may relate to other fields, or start looking into other enterprises. As mentioned earlier, it may require a portfolio of financial activities to cover your gap.

Again, What About You?

- What skills do you have that could be used to bring in income?
- What contacts do you have?
- Do you have skills outside of your profession?
- Do you have a hobby that you could turn into a business?

There is nothing magical or easy in discovering enterprises for income generation, and it is worthwhile to revisit the concept of being *institutionalized* while searching. Do not give credence to the cautions that you cannot return if you leave the work world, or that you will never have a good opportunity again. This is just not true. There is life for you if you leave your work and decide to come back. Many people have had several careers, and it is possible to retire and un-retire over and over again. Had I wanted to move back to Chicago, I could have found a permanent position. I could have even found a permanent position telecommuting from New Mexico. I chose less permanent work because I wanted to retain a degree of independence and only wanted to work enough to fund future adventures. I have continued a pattern of project type work with varying demands on my time for over five years at the time of this writing.

More difficult than finding work will be giving up your independence. It is very hard to get back to taking a business crisis seriously when you have had the freedom to ignore them. Much in the work world will seem so ordinary when you have had the opportunity to do something extraordinary. Because of this you may be better off keeping a semblance of independence (and sanity) by looking at your family, home and lifestyle as your real career. In that way, the projects you take on will be there to allow you to advance your real career rather than to advance through a world you care little about.

Even though I did not give up my independence, it was still an adjustment when I shifted from being completely free from work projects to becoming partially engaged in the work world. Intellectually I knew it was the right thing to do and what I had to do. However, after spending two years away from all forms of work and spending the last five months of that period in the woods while hiking the Appalachian Trail it was still a bit of culture shock to see Dilbert-people actually talking in business jargon with a straight face. When I first heard someone say "collaborative business enterprise" or "core competancies", I almost choked and didn't know if I should start laughing or say *"are you nuts."* Fortunately I have been able to keep my mouth shut, but I still do have to stop myself from blurting out *"who cares."* But by making the necessary adjustments I have been able to fulfill a completely different array of goals. Again I have to say, had we not gone through our initial planning and simplification process we would not have been able to retain our independence for the price of a few compromises.

You may be fortunate to have skills or hobbies that you can translate into income without having to go back to your previous type of work. Regardless of your potential income sources, you will want to retain your network of friends and co-workers. Not only because they are your friends, but when you do want or need to get back involved with work-related activities, they will be the ones who know what you are capable of doing and what might be available for you. As nice as it might be to make a clean break into a new field, the field you know may offer you the best access to income. This does not mean that you cannot develop new skills for an entirely new career or vocation. It just means that, until you have developed a level of expertise in your new field to where someone will actually pay you for it, you may have to rely on what you already know to obtain income. Or, as they say in the entertainment industry, don't quit your day job.

This means that when you leave your job to head for the road, as much as you would like to shred your papers, burn your desk and start singing the Patience and Prudence classic —

> *"...Got along without you before I met you*
> *Gonna get along without you now*
> *So long my honey*
> *Goodbye my dear*
> *Gonna get along without you now"*

DON'T. There is no future in burning your bridges. No matter how well you plan, or how set you may feel right now, things can always change. There are no guarantees, and the bridges behind you may someday become the bridges to your future.

Continuing with the theme of being able to re-connect with the work world if you want or need to, I found that two years out of the workforce was not a hindrance in obtaining work. I found that most people found my on the road experience to be pretty cool and looked at as a positive. As mentioned earlier, it will be the strength of the economy that will have the greatest impact on your finding work. When the economy is strong, there will be plenty of work. When the economy is weak, the projects that would use an outside resource or a new hire will likely be the first to be cut back. This means that in a weak economy you may end up looking harder and, perhaps, taking on lesser work that could pay a lower rate than what you would normally expect. The bottom line is that, if you choose to go on the road and then decide to return to the work world, you can.

The final lesson that I learned in re-connecting with the work world was that the same infrastructure that allowed us to live on the road also allows us to live where we want—in New Mexico. New Mexico has the activities and environment that most appeal to us, but it is not a hot bed of commercial activity with which we are most experienced. It doesn't matter. I can work from my house in New Mexico for a company thousands of miles away. I can accomplish as much as if I were sitting in a desk one cubicle away from you. I can make phone calls. I can email messages and documents to you instantly. I can get a large package to you by tomorrow morning. And again, I can be anywhere or across the street with the same infrastructure that supported us on the road.

WOULD I DO IT AGAIN?

This book is a response to a question, which I have been asked over and over again from the first day I announced my plans to go on the road, of—"*How did you do it?*" The next most frequent

What About Your Overall Health and Being Independent?

I am sure that we all know stress has been identified as a major killer and agree that a reduction in stress will improve ones' health. I would argue that a major cause of stress in our lives is that we are often dependant on so much that we cannot influence. In the corporate world this would be translated into being in a position of responsibility without the authority to manage or even to have access to the necessary resources to meet those responsibilities. As stressful as some job situations may be, there can also be stress in a non-work situation, especially if you do not have enough money to pay your bills, or do not have a meaningful role to play, and are not certain when you can fix the problem. Avoiding stress is perhaps as much about balancing your life as it is about leaving a bad work situation. Because stress is a killer, it is important that your plans for independence have been thought out enough so that you have idea of what you want to do and also have an idea of how to pay for it.

Even though having completely stress-free life may be impossible, declaring your independence can reduce your stress level because making the move to be *on the road* is a decision that is under your control. It is not a decision that has been thrust upon you by an outside force. If you can trust in what you are doing, let go of your fears, and believe that this action can work; a sense of calm can come over you and with that a certain amount of stress will evaporate. This can happen because this is something you have thought through rather than just let happen.

I know in my case that during my last few years in the corporate world I rarely slept the whole night through. I would usually wake up at one or two in the morning and be fully awake. The only way I could get back to sleep was to get out of bed and read or work for the next two or three hours. By the time I got back to sleep, it would then only be an hour or so before the alarm clock would go off, and I would have to get up to go back to work again. When I became independent that problem disappeared within a couple of weeks. If I do find myself getting up in the middle of the night now, I use it as a reminder of what my life used to be like. This for me is stress relief.

With all that being said there is still no immunity from life no matter how stress free your environment. Annoyances and illness can still occur (perhaps on a less frequent basis). In our case, Claudia did need surgery for breast cancer (three years ago at the time of this writing) long after we declared our independence. There is a good chance that the conditions that caused her cancer were present before she declared her independence; nevertheless, she still got sick. She is fine now.

I am not a doctor and do not want to make any health recommendations. You will have to go through your own thought process to determine if an independent course will improve you health.

question I have been asked since doing it is — "*If I could do it all over, would I do it again?*" I can answer that question over seven years later in one word — yes, or if you prefer, two words — absolutely yes. For me, I made the right decision. I wanted to do something different; I did not want to spend the rest of my life in Chicago; and I certainly did not want to spend the rest of my life in the business world. So I did something about it. I can turn the question around and state — could I have done all the things that I have done if I had not declared my independence?

With that being said, life is still life whether you are completely independent or stuck in the worse job in the world. Becoming independent will not all of a sudden make you immune to the realities of life. Stress factors, disappointments, and illnesses will still rear their ugly heads. There is no special formula or magical remedy for happiness that will appear just because you stepped out onto a different path. Life is not about "*good things will happen for me because I am good*" that you chant over and over again in a mantra. Life is just life, and the responsibility of finding the balance between resignation and intervention is not going to disappear regardless of how happy or unhappy you are with some of your decisions. Sometimes no matter what — stuff happens.

What works for me may or may not work for you. What I hope you gather from the arguments presented in this book is that ordinary people can do something extraordinary, and that the choice to do or not to do something about it is your decision and not someone else's. Do your homework, do your self examination, and then follow a course that is right for you.

RETAINING YOUR INDEPENDENCE
AFTER SHIFTING GEARS

As I just stated, I am glad I had extended time on the road, and have worked hard at retaining a semblance of independence since being domiciled. As I also stated, most people who have had a taste of being independent really do not relish going back to the corporate world. If you are not independently wealthy or on a healthy pension, you will have to be involved in some form of work or enterprise to finance some phases of your on-the-road experience. Some form of self-employment, occasional work or personal enterprise will be your most likely path for retaining some semblance of independence.

We have already discussed that when you established an infrastructure for the road you have also established an infrastructure for supporting a home-based business. We have also discussed that your future work could very well likely have a connection to your past. If your experience has been entirely as an employee, there will be some items that may be new to you as the proprietor of a home based enterprise. They include:

Taxes

As a self-employed businessperson or contractor you will become familiar with completing a Schedule C on your federal income tax return and paying Self-Employment Taxes. The Schedule C is for reporting you business income and expenses to determine how much money you actually made for tax purposes. Self-Employment Tax is the equivalent of the Social Security Tax that you paid when you were employed. The only difference now is that you will be responsible for both your share and your employer's share of the tax, or about double what you paid as an employee. Another tax issue is that you will no longer have an employer withholding money from your paycheck. If you want to avoid penalties for late payment you will want to make quarterly Estimated Income Tax payments. More information on these and other tax issues are available from the IRS and your state department of revenue.

Pricing Your Services

Because you will now be buying your own health insurance, paying Self-Employment Tax, and maintaining your own office it is important to understand the relative value of the work that you will be taking on compared to that of a salaried individual. For example, $25 per hour, on the surface, may look like a $50,000 a year job (40 hours per week * $25 per hour = $1000 week * 50 weeks = $50,000 annually). It's not. The salaried individual who is making $50,000 a year is also receiving paid holidays, sick days and vacation time. If you take away the time spent on vacations and holidays, that salaried person is probably only working 47 weeks per year. If you, as a contractor, take the same holidays and vacation time, your 47 weeks of work will bring in $47,000 rather than $50,000. Furthermore, the salaried individual will be paying only their half of Social Security tax. As a self-employed contractor you will pay both halves of Social Security (Self-Employment Tax). This will reduce your $47,000 by another $2000 to $3000 or so to around $45,000. Depending on your line of work you will be incurring the cost of tools and infrastructure that will further reduce your income. The salaried individual will most likely be receiving benefits (medical insurance, 401(k) match, and others) which you will not have. Those benefits would conservatively be worth at least ten percent of that salaried employee's base salary, or $5,000. The salaried person is now receiving the equivalent of at least $55,000 to your $45,000. That $45,000 would be reduced by your expense for tools and benefits.

This is more than a twenty percent difference in an apparent hourly rate and the actual cost of an employee. This means that you will not be out of line to ask for $30 per hour rather than $25 per hour for work that would normally be done by a $50,000 a year salaried individual. In fact, you could be justified in asking for more because the company will not have the hiring, termination, office, training, development or management expenses that are normally associated with most regular employees. By using your services the firm hiring you will be able to limit their financial exposure only to work that needs to be done. They will not be responsible for figuring out what to do with you during slow periods or to pay you during those times. In short, you will be a bargain for the firm hiring you.

All that being said, what you can expect to receive for work on a contract or consulting basis will be determined by what is available to you and what a company is willing to pay you for the work. Just because you may think of yourself as a $50,000 a year, or $100,000 a year or more per year worker does not mean that you will always obtain work at that level. The only thing that really matters is how the work fits into your strategy for covering "the gap", or for providing personal enrichment.

Time Allocation

How your work fits into your personal strategy leads to another consideration—how do you allocate your time between projects for income and those for personal enrichment? The more you can control and reduce the size of "the gap", the less time you will need to spend on projects for income. Along the same lines, the more work you can do at a higher billing rate, the more time you can spend on projects for personal enrichment. If you do not properly manage "the gap" and also fail to obtain work at an adequate billing rate, then all you may have done in leaving your job is to trade one work experience for another. On the other hand, if your main reason for going on the road was to adopt a completely different lifestyle or career, you will be financially successful if your new endeavor, or combination of endeavors, generates enough money to cover the gap regardless of how many hours it takes.

If your purpose for engaging in income-producing projects is to cover the gap and to leave adequate time for other interests, you will want to look at the nature of the work and expected income from the work very closely. In that case you may want a steady part-time activity, or you might want periods of being fully engaged in a work endeavor to accumulate a surplus. The surplus would then be used to fund future activities, or periods without income generating activities. What you do not want is to find yourself doing work that you do not particularly like, that does not pay enough to cover the gap, and then takes all of your time. If that is the case, welcome to the world of the working poor.

To avoid that unpleasantness you should consider categorizing different levels of income producing activities as to their desirability. You will have to use your experience to assign an approximate dollar value for each of these categories. For instance, you may look at $25 per hour as higher paying while someone else may consider it lower paying. Work activity categories to consider could be:

- Work or an activity that is so desirable that you would pay to do it if you could. This is really something that should be moved to the category of personal enrichment and should not be considered a financial endeavor.

- Lower paying, but somewhat interesting, task that you would do as a favor for a friend, or to occupy some idle time, or something that would allow you to spend time in a place that you really like. This again should not be considered a financial endeavor and should be looked at as an opportunity to generate some walking around money.

The important thing to recognize in the previous two activities is that if your gap is minimal or non-existent, then these may be all the project categories you need or care to do. On the other hand if your gap is larger and will take some effort to cover, then you really need to make sure that these "fun" type projects do not overcrowd your dance card. For those with a larger gap, additional categories would include:

- Work that pays in the middle range is worth doing to help manage the gap while waiting for a better or more interesting opportunity to come along. It is important to recognize that this type of work is only allowing you to get along rather than to get ahead. The difficulty with this type of work is that even if you do it fulltime, there will most likely be an insufficient carryover to fund many other new and more interesting activities.

- Obviously, work that is higher paying is the most desirable in managing the gap because it allows you to make more money in fewer hours to provide more time for more interesting activities. The other advantage of a higher paying endeavor is that there could be enough money involved to make it worth your while to work fulltime for a while to build up a surplus to fund future activities.

Other motivations in considering work options besides managing the gap may be to remain involved and to make a contribution when there are lulls or downtime in your various activities. Keeping your bandwidth full is never a bad idea.

Time/Price Allocation

If you are taking on jobs to cover the gap, it is important to make sure that the mix is sufficient to cover the gap and to fulfill your reasons for choosing the road. For example, let's say your gap is $25,000 a year. This means that you will need to bring in approximately $500 per week to cover the gap. If you are making around $12.50 an hour, you would need to work fulltime to cover the gap. If you can up your rate to around $25 an hour, you would then only need to work twenty hours a week to cover the gap. At this point you can start mixing it up with both income and personal enrichment projects. If you are able to make more, you are now in a position to look at reducing your hours or increasing your surplus to fund another time off period. Again, this will all be dependant upon what is currently available to you and how you blend them together.

Managing the "Tar Baby" Project

As you obtain projects, some will better than others. Some may be more interesting or pay better. But lurking out there can be real "tar babies" where no matter how hard you struggle the more you will get stuck. A "tar baby" project can sometimes feel worse than a fulltime permanent job. Your job will be to manage it so that it does not ruin your life or to figure out how to extricate yourself from the trap.

Oftentimes a "tar baby" is the result of your role in the project drifting away from providing a specific deliverable to a role with more managerial or coordination responsibilities. Sometimes a "tar baby" is the result of a "24 by 7" corporate culture where an impromptu late evening or weekend business meeting is the norm. The first step in managing the situation is to remember that it does not have to be forever. Just like you can change jobs, you can always leave a project. You just want to do it gracefully. As for dealing with expanded responsibilities or a high-stress corporate culture, the best defense is to focus on what you have been asked to deliver and to deliver it when promised.

You do have another advantage in managing an unpleasant project when you are working from home. You are not in the office where they can see you. You can create the appearance of being available "24 by 7" by being responsive to what needs to be done and delivering what you promised when you promised. For every assignment, you should make sure that you have a clear definition of what is expected and when it is needed. You may occasionally have to work some strange hours, but if you can consistently be responsive no one will care or question how or when you are using your time. Remember that you are being paid for your results and not for your life. So as long as you deliver results, you can keep your life.

Appreciate What You Are Able to Get

As stated many times, part of becoming independent is to change your mindset from an employee to an entrepreneur. As an employee, you would expect to be paid so much per week for so many hours on the job per week regardless of how busy you were. As an entrepreneur, you will only earn what you actually brought in that week. So if you are currently only working part time, or at a lower rate, be happy with what you brought in that week to help cover the gap. Measure what you get rather than what you did not get. If those lesser hours or lower rate are not meeting your objectives, place your energies in fixing the problem rather feeling bad about it. Keep in mind that with a simplified life and a manageable gap, a period of a lower run rate will not be the same disaster as it would have been when you had a higher income requirement.

Working as an Outsider

If you have never worked as an outsider, your primary adjustment will be to understand that your role now is a service provider rather than an employee. You are there to complete a series of tasks or assignments efficiently and effectively to help make the project that you are assisting a success. You are not there to be a big-shot. If you want to be a big-shot, and that's okay, you would be better served by seeking permanent employment as a decision maker, or buying or starting your own business. Your satisfaction as an outside service provider will come from knowing that you have been of help, while at the same time furthering your own personal agenda.

There could be times when you may have more experience on a matter and have a better perspective than those who have engaged your services. This could open the door to personal frustration if you perceive them as running in the wrong direction or making a series of serious mistakes. No matter how difficult, you need to recognize that you have not been engaged to tell them what total idiots they are. You really do need to step back and remember that you are there to use your abilities to deliver on your assignments. In doing so, your efforts may help mollify the impact of poor decision making and in the process further increase the value of your contribution.

Over time you will find that one of the better benefits of working on a temporary or consulting basis is being an outsider. Other than its impact on the need for your services, you no longer need to worry about who got what promotion or what changes HR has in store for the employee benefits package. It's just not your concern, and there is no benefit to you in getting caught up in office politics and bickering. An employee has every right to pound on their desk about things not being done right and a legitimate amount of griping is expected from an employee. An outsider does not have that luxury. Your job is to serve the person hiring you and to contribute as best you can. Fighting battles and implementing reform is their concern, not yours. Once you make this adjustment, a certain sense of calmness can come over you, and with that you can become even more valuable to those who hire you by being a positive force within a raging sea of negativity and discouragement.

The final thing to recognize as an outsider is that you are not necessarily there to make a "career." You are there to cover "the gap", to help out, to fund additional adventures, or to learn. You can have the satisfaction of knowing that every dollar you earn is a contribution to your own private agenda. The more you can blend into what is happening around you the easier it will be for you to move in and out of the shadows as your income requirements ebb and flow.

A perspective of an outsider can also help make "lesser" work more palatable. As mentioned earlier, a fear of many who have been *institutionalized* is that they could end up flipping burgers. A more positive approach would be to adopt the attitude that flipping burgers is honest and honorable work, which it is. It is even easier to take on that attitude knowing that it is contributing to your overall life agenda, which it might also be.

Example of Balancing "Lesser" Work with Your Overall Agenda

Three years ago I was in a situation where Claudia had had surgery, and I wanted to be available to help her recover and not be engaged in a demanding work situation. A friend of mine, who was in charge of a sales force at the time, asked me if I could go through a database they had to identify potential sales leads. The task essentially involved "cold calling" several hundred companies to interview them to find out their current situation and determine if they could be a good candidate for my friend's product. If you have been in a sales position, you know that "cold calling" is essential but undesirable work. It is a task you would gladly see performed by someone else. It was a task that would certainly be "lesser" to what I had done when I was employed and "lesser" than what I had done in other contract/consulting situations.

I readily accepted the offer for many reasons. It was something that my experience would allow me to do and deliver good results. It was something that I could do from home so I could be available to help Claudia in her recovery. It was something I could do three or four hours a day to bring in enough money to keep "the gap" under control. Because it would only take three or four hours a day, it was something that would not be interfering with my other projects.

One of the salespeople at my friend's company asked me if I was content making "cold calls" with my background. I replied that the work was not a problem for me because it was work that needed to be done and that it was something I would not be doing forever. I also pointed out that the results were helping him do his job better. I also mentioned that it worked for me because it was not interfering with what I preferred to be doing. At the same time that I was making calls I was attending an archaeology class at the University of New Mexico two days a week and working on a book on the Appalachian Trail that was subsequently published and has had some modest success. The "cold calling" engagement was not "lesser" work; it was what was allowing me meet my responsibilities and to continue to do other things.

I can further say that the book on the Appalachian Trail has been more important to me and has given me more satisfaction than anything I ever did in a business role, whether "higher" or "lesser." I have received many emails from readers, even two years after the book came out, thanking me for writing the book and for helping them do something extraordinary in their life. Connecting with a complete stranger and making a positive impact in their life has been more important to me than any corporate job I ever had. And again, if I had not changed my path, this could not have happened. The ability to experiment and do something different is another reason for me to choose the road.

Apprenticeship

If your intention for going on the road is to learn a new skill or to change careers, you will probably have to go through an apprenticeship (or initiation) process. You cannot expect potential new colleagues, who have spent much of their adult life in the field, to embrace you as an equal just because you showed up. Taking a continuing education class in your new field or reading a book about it will not make you an instant expert or give you credibility. Unless your new field has been a lifelong interest or hobby, you may have to do your best to cram a lifetime of learning into a short timeframe to be able to participate in your new field. It will only be through hard and high quality work that you will be able to show your new colleagues that you are worthy of their respect. Because an apprenticeship may take some time, you may need to continue to do work in your prior field until your expertise in your new field is at a level where someone would actually pay you for it.

Entrepreneurial Enterprise

Others of you may have chosen the road in order to relocate to new area with the idea of setting up your own enterprise(s). Earlier in the book I mentioned that investment opportunities tend to be local. Entrepreneurial opportunities are also local. You may have to live in an area for a while before you are able to identify opportunities that would be of interest to you and that you are capable of handling. In your search, you may meet people who are occupying a niche that you find appealing. Do not expect them to greet you with open arms and say — "*welcome brother and let's do a project together.*" Chances are that in their minds, they see their pie as being barely large enough to feed them, let alone large enough to cut off a slice to share with you. This does not mean that you cannot learn from them or that they will be adversarial to you. It just means that your own entrepreneurial enterprise will be like any other business in that you must demonstrate that you bring enough value to the table for someone else to be interested in doing business with you. No one is going to give away their "*sunshine hole*" (a sure thing) to you. Nor can you look up "*sunshine holes*" in the yellow pages or want ads to find one. You will have to go out and develop your own. Again, just as in any career change, you may need to continue to do work in a field where you have the most expertise. With that being said, you should keep at it and not give up.

SUMMARY

Again, I cannot say it enough, there is life after leaving the conventional work world, and it can be good. If you achieve the right blend of personal projects and financial projects it can even be better. There are many things you can do beyond flipping burgers. You just have to be realistic about what you can do and what you can get. And further remember, if it fits within your overall strategy, even so-called "lesser" work can play an important role in your strategy.

Conclusion

New Mexico back country.
Photograph by the author.

"Do not be one of those who, rather than risk failure, never attempts anything."

New Seeds of Contemplation — Thomas Merton

I cannot walk your path or tell you what to do. I cannot tell you if you should change. I can only say that I am glad I chose a path that allowed me to have a two-year adventure on the road and more independent existence since leaving the road. I hope that I have shown that a different existence might be possible for you. If you think you should change and have nothing stopping you from changing but are still on the fence, you might want to ask yourself if you are going in the same direction as *George Babbitt*, the main character from Sinclair Lewis' 1922 satire.

Babbitt concludes with George's son Ted announcing to his family his plans to live differently than what they had expected. In an effort to change Ted's mind, George and Ted have gone to the dining room to confer privately. Instead of changing Ted's mind, George makes the following confession in the final page of the book,

> "Well —" Babbitt crossed the floor, slowly, ponderously, seem-ing a little old. "I've always wanted you to have a college degree." He meditatively stamped across the floor again. "But I've never — Now, for heaven's sake, don't repeat this to your mother, or she'd remove what little hair I've got left, but practically, **I've never**

done a single thing I've wanted to in my whole life! I don't know's I've accomplished anything except **just get along.** I figure out I've made about a quarter of an inch out of a possible hundred rods. Well, maybe you'll carry things on further. I don't know. But I do get a kind of sneaking pleasure out of the fact that you knew what you wanted to do and did it. Well, those folks in there will try and bully you, and tame you down. Tell 'em to go to the devil! I'll back you. Take your factory job, if you want to. Don't be scared of the family. No, nor all of Zenith. Nor of yourself, the way I've been. Go ahead, old man! The world is yours!"

Arms about each other shoulders, the Babbitt men marched into the living-room and faced the swooping family.

Whether you choose independence or not, ask yourself if you might be living the life of George Babbitt. Are you just getting along and doing nothing that you have ever wanted to do? Have you considered the possibility of balancing your responsibilities to include doing what you want to do?

If you are reluctant to declare your independence, keep in mind that by not acting you are making a bet. You are betting that you will still be alive and that your health and energy level will still be what it is today if you wait. You are also betting that the opportunities available to you today will still be there for you if you wait. But ultimately it is your right to make that bet, and it is your life and your choice on how you live it. Each one of us is responsible for the lives we lead.

Afterword

"Life is not a problem to be solved,
but a reality to be experienced."

Soren Kierkegaard

My original intention was to write a book on how to actually live and make a life for yourself on the road. As I made progress on the book, I kept setting it to the side because it did not seem relevant. Not everyone wants to, or can actually live on the road like Claudia and I did. If they did, they are more than likely fulltime RVers and most likely don't need a book from me on how to do it. I also realized that it has been several years since Claudia and I actually lived on the road and that we have moved on to other experiences. As I am sure you have gathered from reading this book, our literal time on the road was a truly great experience for us, but maybe not for you.

But what did hit me as I kept coming back to this project is that I am not independently wealthy but have not had to seek a permanent job to keep the lights burning. I have been able to find enough income producing activities to cover "the gap" without sacrificing time for learning or pursuing activities that have been more personally rewarding to me than any paycheck I ever received. Also the income-producing activities and circumstances that allowed me to leave my job over seven years ago have changed over the years, yet I have still been able to maintain a large degree of independence.

I began to realize that the planning process that we went through and the approaches in our thinking (or, to use today's cliché — willingness to step out of the box) are what made it possible for us to live on the road and to retain a sense of independence. I also realized that there are now many people who are reaching a point in their life where they need to come to grips with the fact that they are not getting younger, and that it may be the time for them to rethink their priorities and truly decide what they want to get out of their life. In addition to the clock not stopping, the changes in our economy and the resulting dislocation are also not stopping. In fact, they seem to be accelerating. Companies continue to downsize, job losses due to mergers and acquisitions are reported almost every day in the newspaper, many skill-sets have left the country, and the future of Social Security seems less certain. The list goes on. It may be that one's best course of defense against this onslaught is to separate oneself from the noise and declare personal independence. That is, not only stepping out of the box, but also mentally moving off the grid.

I came back to this book and finished it because I finally realized that I may have something to say that could be helpful to someone considering or facing independence. I also came back to this book because there are many people who are fed up with their current lot and do relate to the opening quote and do want to *check out of their bourgeois motel and say no more jell-o for me*. I finished it because they may need help in their planning and decision-making process. I believe that it is important for people who feel this way to realize that they are not alone and that their struggle with *normalcy* has been the subject of literature for hundreds of years, if not thousands. I also believe that a strong argument can be made that much of current life is unnatural, and that their struggle is legitimate. Even if someone does not relate to the opening quote, they still may be looking at the prospect of forced independence. They too may need help in their planning and decision-making. I hope this book has further relevance in showing others that there are other paths, though not necessarily easy, to follow, and that the extraordinary is available to the ordinary. If you are ready for change and do not relish the prospect of the rest of your life being consigned to a corporate existence, Claudia and I are proof that it is does not have to be that way.

Resource Guide

REE & EASY: *How to Create Your Own Adventure by Living on the Road* is a compilation of what we have absorbed and learned over the years about personal independence. The book, however, is not a precise template for what you should do. For that you will have to do your own research and make your own decisions. Your research could include further exploring many of the topics and ideas brought up in the book. Some items to consider include:

Financial Management

Resources for learning about how to manage your investments and basic financial principals can be found in your local bookstore and on the Internet. I have found the following web pages to be especially helpful.

- *www.berkshirehathaway.com* — Warren Buffet (the nation's most successful investor) issues an annual letter to the shareholders of Berkshire Hathaway (his company) every March. The letter summarizes his observations on the current state of the economy. His most recent letter and previous letters can be found on the Berkshire Hathaway web page.

- *www.bobbrinker.com* — Bob Brinker is the host of the syndicated weekend radio program — *MoneyTalk*. Bob Brinker's web page provides information and links to other sites that can provide you with a thorough education in managing your money.

- *www.cbsmarketwatch.com* — CBS MarketWatch provides a web page for daily financial news and personal financial planning. I have found the articles by Paul B. Farrell to be very helpful. They offer good common sense advice and are presented from a philosophical perspective. His articles can be found under the Personal Finance tab of the web page. Past articles have been archived and many are still relevant and well worth reading.

Taxes

Federal tax forms and tax publications (including Publication 590 — Individual Retirement Arrangements IRAs) can be found on the IRS web page — *www.irs.gov.*

Personal Health

The focus of **Free and Easy: How to Create Your Own Adventure by Living on the Road** is about making the decision to have an independent life. Although a healthy lifestyle goes hand in hand with a simplified independent life, the book does not go into any depth regarding personal health and lifestyle choices. This is for good reason as there are many excellent sources of information regarding these choices. Among them is Dr. Andrew Weil who has written many books, including **Eating Well for Optimum Heath** (Alfred A. Knopf, New York, 2000). The book provides in-depth information on nutrition, health, and healing for an improved overall lifestyle. The book includes many recipes for preparing healthy meals. Dr. Weil maintains a comprehensive web page on a holistic approach towards a healthy life — *www.drweil.com.* When you access his web page you can sign up for his email newsletter and receive a *DailyTip from Dr. Weil* in your email inbox every day.

Simplification

As stated in the text, those who are not independently wealthy or are without a guaranteed income may have to engage in some form of simplification in order to declare personal independence. If you are interested in learning more about simplification you can read **Your Money or Your Life** by Joe Dominguez and Vicki Robin (Viking, New York, 1992). You can also find information on the Internet by searching on voluntary simplicity, simple living, life simplification, or similar terms. *Simpleliving.net* is affiliated with **Your Money or Your Life;** while *www.simpleliving.com* is affiliated with **Simple Living** magazine. You will have to make your own decision on how simplification applies to you.

To Think About

There are many concepts and ideas presented in this book that you may wish to examine further. Among them are:

- The book **Walden** by Henry David Thoreau is a chronicle of Thoreau's experiment in self-sufficient living at Walden Pond from 1845 to 1847 (see page 5 and 8). The book is readily available at bookstores and libraries.

- The writings of Thomas Merton are a discussion of choosing a life of understanding and contemplation (see pages 5 and 8). Merton was called to a Trappist monastery in 1941 at the age of 26. There he wrote, and over the years he expanded his level of awareness to incorporate teachings from a diversity of backgrounds. He died in an accident in Asia in 1968 while on a tour to open doors to other religious traditions. Noted books include **Seven Story Mountain, New Seeds of Contemplation,** and **The Asian Journal of Thomas Merton.** They are still in print and widely available.

- The concept of "institutionalized" is used throughout the book (see page 21). To see an application and inspiration of the concept you can watch the 1994 prison movie **The Shawshank Redemption** starring Morgan Freeman and Tim Robbins. It is based upon a Steven King novella.

- I mentioned in the book (see page 42) that Richard Halliburton was a 1930's era adventurer. While in college he decided to spend a life of adventure rather than take a normal job, and for most of the 1920's and 1930's he managed to do everything conceivable until he did not return from his final adventure in 1939. His books were quite popular in his time and include **The Royal Road to Romance** and **Seven League Boots.** The books are long out of print and quite dated. If you can find them, they are still fun to read.

- To appreciate the spirit behind the quote *the maximum is not the optimum* (see page 64) you can find it in Garrett Hardin's 1968 essay *The Tragedy of the Commons.* The essay is available on the Internet at *www.garrethardin society.org.*

- You were given a homework assignment (see page 71) to watch the 1985 Albert Brooks comedy **Lost in America.** You should have learned of the necessity of protecting your nest egg to ensure that you keep your independence.

- Although the 1993 movie **Groundhog Day** (see page 95) (staring Bill Murray) about a man having to repeat the same day over and over again has been billed as a romantic comedy; it is really a portrayal of one man's journey towards enlightenment and of finally getting it right (learning). The movie has been the subject of many scholarly essays and has been studied by many teachers from a variety of religious backgrounds. If you have not seen it, it is well worth making the time to watch it. The story (and screenplay) is by Danny Rubin.

- I mentioned the desirability of not joining the working poor (see page 135). That is, performing work that is not particularly compelling, takes all of your time, and does not pay enough to cover the bills. If you are interested in learning more about the plight of the working poor and what it is like to cope in that situation, you can find more information in **Nickel and Dimed** by Barbara Ehrenreich (Henry Holt and Company, New York, 2001).

- While discussing overseas travel, I mentioned that most of the vagabonds and trekkers you meet are from Europe or Australia (see page 108). This is primarily because of shorter vacations and a different attitude towards work in America. More information on this topic is discussed in **The Overworked American** by Juliet B. Schor (HarperCollins, New York, 1992).

- In discussing establishing enterprises for sources of income to cover "the gap", I mentioned that this is not necessarily easy to do, nor will you find *sunshine holes* in the Yellow Pages to make the task unnecessary (see page 142). To help you identify and establish a personal enterprise you can read **How to Make a Living Without a Job** by Barbara J. Winter (Bantam Books, New York,

1993). The book is compilation of what she has learned from conducting workshops and classes in establishing a home-based business.

- After completing the manuscript for **Free and Easy,** I came across **Too Young to Retire** by Marika and Howard Stone (Penguin Group, New York, 2002). The Stones are proprietors of the web page *www.2young2retire.com.* Their web site offers many suggestions on how to live an active and enterprising life well past the age of a "traditional" retirement. The book has many good ideas and points you toward many opportunities to consider.

- If you are interested in learning more about the possibility of the "traditional" retirement being impractical and perhaps undesirable in many cases, you can find more information in **The Retirement Myth** by Craig S. Karpel (Harper Collins, New York, 1995). As the title implies, the book does have a bit of a doom and gloom edge, but it does offer much to think about in your overall strategy for independence.

- While in the stage of starting and stopping the manuscript for **Free and Easy,** I came across **Free Agent Nation: The Future of Working for Yourself** by Daniel Pink (Warner Books, New York, 2002). The book describes a trend of more and more people doing project type work as opposed to having permanent employment. His book mentions many of the same infrastructural items that I have used in my independence as being useful for project work.

- Although I do not use the term *follow your bliss* in the book, the book is to a great extent very much about following your bliss. The term was coined by Joseph Campbell who wrote many books about the power of myth and human experience. In his PBS interview with Bill Moyers first aired in 1988 (shortly after his death), he cites the story of George Babbitt about never doing anything he wanted (see page 147). More information on Joseph Campbell can be found on the Joseph Campbell Foundation web page — *www.jcf.org*. The full six hours of the PBS **Joseph Campbell and Power of Myth** interviews with Bill Moyers are available for purchase from bookstores or PBS.

ABOUT THE AUTHOR

David Ryan and his wife Claudia were able to leave their corporate jobs for a more independent existence over seven years ago when he was 49 and she was 48 without the benefit of an inheritance, corporate buyout, severance package, pension, huge windfall, or a winning lottery ticket. They were able to create their own adventure through their ability to recognize and organize the resources available to them. His book *Free and Easy: How to Create Your Own Adventure by Living on the Road* describes the thought process that went into making this happen and shares what they learned while on the road. The author uses the expression *on the road* as a metaphor for bringing change into your life. His previous book **Long Distance Hiking on the Appalachian Trail for the Older Adventurer** is an introduction to the long-distance hiking experience. Both books are about how the extraordinary can be available to the ordinary.

The author was born in Evanston, Illinois in 1947, grew up in the Chicago area, and graduated from the University of Denver in 1969. He has two daughters, Jennifer and Amy, who are both in their early 30's. Most of his adult life prior to independence was spent in Chicago where he was employed in various sales, marketing and analyst positions in the Information Technology (IT) industry. Prior to the IT industry, the author had a brief stint as a minor league baseball executive in the early 1970's.

After leaving the corporate world David and Claudia embarked on a series of personal adventures that kept them literally on the road for two years. One of them was hiking the entire length of the 2160-mile Appalachian Trail. They now live in New Mexico, where he is still a White Sox fan, with their three dogs. There they have pursued a different array of activities and continue to maintain their independence.

CONTACT INFORMATION

Contact the Author:
David Ryan
612–889–9640
E-Mail: davidryan@msn.com
Fax: 928–222–0022
Website: www.newmountainbooks.com

ORDERING INFORMATION

Call-in your order: 505–982–0066
Fax: 505–982–6858
or Write:

Pennywhistle Press
1807 Second Street, Suite 28
Santa Fe, NM 87505
E-Mail: pennywhistlebook@aol.com
Website: www.pennywhistlepress.com